• Myths of Light •

The Collected Works of Joseph Campbell

Thou Art That:
Transforming Religious Metaphor

The Inner Reaches of Outer Space:
Metaphor as Myth and as Religion

The Flight of the Wild Gander: Selected Essays 1944–1968

The Hero's Journey:
Joseph Campbell on His Life and Work

Myths of Light:
Eastern Metaphors of the Eternal

Mythic Worlds, Modern Words:
Joseph Campbell on the Art of James Joyce

Pathways to Bliss:
Mythology and Personal Transformation

A Skeleton Key to Finnegans Wake:
Unlocking James Joyce's Masterwork

The Mythic Dimension: Selected Essays 1959–1987

The Hero with a Thousand Faces

Mythic Imagination: Collected Short Fiction

Goddesses: Mysteries of the Feminine Divine

Romance of the Grail: The Magic and Mystery of Arthurian Myth

Asian Journals: India and Japan

The Ecstasy of Being: Mythology and Dance

More titles forthcoming

JOSEPH CAMPBELL

· Myths of Light ·

EASTERN METAPHORS OF THE ETERNAL

Edited and with a foreword by David Kudler

JOSEPH CAMPBELL™
FOUNDATION

New World Library
Novato, California

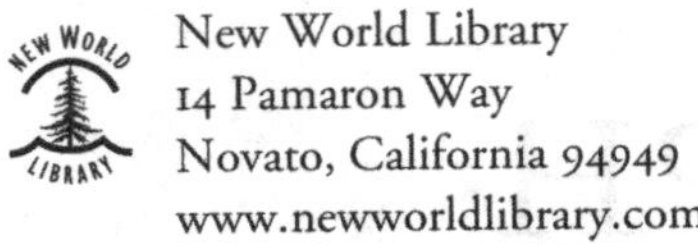

New World Library
14 Pamaron Way
Novato, California 94949
www.newworldlibrary.com

Cover design by Mary Ann Casler
Text design and typography by Tona Pearce Myers

Grateful acknowledgment is made to The British Museum for the permission to reprint the following images: Steatite seal from the Indus Valley on page 13; stele with Kirtimukha above on page 23; footprints of the Buddha on page 32; Visnu sheltered by the cosmic serpent Ananta on page 82; Taking a lute to visit a friend, attributed to Jiang Song, on page 85. All images are copyright © The British Museum. Grateful acknowledgment is made to the Internet Sacred Text Archive for the following images: Kali on page 51; and Visnu, Brahma, and Laksmi on page 55. Both images copyright © The Internet Sacred Text Archive (www.sacred-texts.com).

Library of Congress Cataloging-in-Publication Data
Campbell, Joseph, 1904–1987
Myths of light : Eastern metaphors of the eternal / by Joseph Campbell ; edited and with a foreword by David Kudler.
p. cm. — (Collected works of Joseph Campbell)
Includes bibliographical references and index.
ISBN 978-1-57731-403-5 (hardcover : alk. paper)
1. Mythology, Asian. 2. Asia—Religion. I. Kudler, David. II. Title.
BL1033.C36 2003
291.1'3'095—dc21 2003003878

First paperback printing, April 2012
ISBN 978-1-60868-109-9
Printed in Canada on 100% postconsumer-waste recycled paper

New World Library is proud to be a Gold Certified Environmentally Responsible Publisher. Publisher certification awarded by Green Press Initiative.
www.greenpressinitiative.org

10 9 8 7 6 5 4 3

CONTENTS

ABOUT THE COLLECTED WORKS OF JOSEPH CAMPBELL

At his death in 1987, Joseph Campbell left a significant body of published work that explored his lifelong passion, the complex of universal myths and symbols that he called "Mankind's one great story." He also left, however, a large volume of unreleased work: uncollected articles, notes, letters, and diaries, as well as audio- and videotape recorded lectures.

The Joseph Campbell Foundation was founded in 1991 to preserve, protect, and perpetuate Campbell's work. The Foundation has undertaken to archive his papers and recordings in digital format, and to publish previously unavailable material and out-of-print works as *The Collected Works of Joseph Campbell.*

THE COLLECTED WORKS OF JOSEPH CAMPBELL
Robert Walter, Executive Editor
David Kudler, Managing Editor

EDITOR'S FOREWORD

By the time Joseph Campbell returned from his yearlong journey to Asia in 1955, he had undergone a literally life-changing experience. Since his chance meeting with Jiddu Krishnamurti on a transatlantic liner in 1924, Campbell had been fascinated with the myths and religions of what was then universally known as the Orient. During his graduate studies in Europe, he had been introduced to the ideas of Western thinkers such as C. G. Jung, Adolph Bastian, and the Romantic philosophers of the nineteenth century, all of whom had been profoundly influenced by Oriental thought and imagery.

In 1942, as a professor at Sarah Lawrence College, he had the good fortune to become a friend and protégé of the great Indologist Heinrich Zimmer, whose ideas on the mythic underpinnings of the Indian religions enriched and informed his own views. When Zimmer died in 1945, Campbell agreed with Zimmer's widow, Christiane, that he would edit the notes and unfinished work that Zimmer had left behind. This endeavor had filled Campbell's professional life until his year of travel, when he at last came face-to-face with the continent that he had read and written so much about.

Of course, the Asia he experienced was both infinitely more and infinitely less than he had expected. His journals of this journey, which have been published as *Baksheesh & Brahman* and *Sake & Satori,* resonate with his frustration, but also with his wonder. While he was disappointed with what he found to be an emphasis on what the Indians call *bhakti,* ritual devotion, he was also astonished with a mode of thought—evident in Calcutta and Kyoto, Bengal and Bangkok—that was fundamentally different from the Western mode in which Campbell himself had been raised. It was a mind-set that assumed an altogether different connection between the individual and the transcendent. Instead of the relationship of creature to Creator, Campbell found cultures that defined the self as being identical with the eternal—that which Hindus call *Brahman.*

Campbell found this approach remarkably refreshing. Talking about how Japanese culture lacked the concept of the Fall of Man, Campbell said, "I've told friends to save their money on psychotherapy and visit Japan."

The other major revelation that struck Campbell during this trip was the absolute lack of education in comparative mythology and religion that afflicted most Americans. Throughout the trip, he was embarrassed to observe fellow countrymen—even among the scholars and diplomats he traveled with—who were either woefully ill informed about or utterly indifferent to the cultures they encountered.

These two thoughts combined to inspire Campbell to transform his career. No longer would he be content to limit himself to writing for his peers and teaching only his students. Strictly speaking, he had intended *The Hero with a Thousand Faces,* published in 1949, to be a popular work, as we can see from its original title, *How to Read a Myth.* Nevertheless, it had been, to that point, a niche publication, not yet having gained the wide influence it would come to wield in American pop culture. Now, Campbell began consciously to seek ways to reach a broader audience. He undertook—while still in Asia—to write a popular overview of comparative myth. The result was his four-volume masterpiece, *The Masks of God,* a comprehensive history of religion and myth that appeared between 1959 and 1968.

His other major enterprise was a series of lectures, in conferences, churches, State Department halls, and finally on radio and television. These lectures were always intended to enlighten American audiences about both their own traditions and the larger world of myth and symbol. To our great benefit, Campbell began to record these lectures, for his own use in preparing his books. (Always at his best as an impromptu speaker, Campbell delivered most of these lectures without notes.)

A favorite topic, from his return to the United States to his death in 1987, was the mythology of the great Indian and East Asian religions. The Joseph Campbell Foundation archives list hundreds of lectures on subjects broad and esoteric, but focused on the world that Campbell resolutely called the Orient.

This book is drawn almost entirely from transcripts of those lectures, along with some unpublished essays. In each, Campbell explores the Eastern metaphors of the eternal by their many names: *Brahman,* the Tao, the Buddha mind.

The first chapter, "The Birth of *Brahman,*" focuses on the essence of the idea of that transcendent World Soul and its historical development. The second chapter, "The Jīva's Journey," looks at the relationship of that idea to the view of the individual in Indian and East Asian traditional culture. The penultimate chapter, "Vessels to the Farther Shore," examines the particular modes in which the idea of the transcendent has clothed itself in the East—that is, the various religions and how they have developed throughout the region and throughout history.

In preparing to edit this work, I was faced with many challenges. The first was to decide what material to include. I had just finished assisting in the completion of the first volume in this current series, *Thou Art That: Transforming Religious Metaphor,* edited by Eugene Kennedy, which focused on the underlying myths of the Judeo-Christian tradition. It seemed that a similar book that represented a parallel exploration of Asian myths was in order.

I reviewed as much of Campbell's work on Asian mythology—both published and unpublished—as I could, and began to concentrate on the idea that is now examined in this volume. Once the basic thesis was set, I knew that I would use seven lectures that have been released as part of *The Joseph Campbell Audio Collection*—two from the volume entitled "The Inward Journey: East and West" and the five that make up the volume

"The Eastern Way." Campbell made all of these recordings during his first great round of public teaching in the 1960s. I then scoured through the other lecture transcripts and unpublished writings that Campbell left behind, and found many that filled what I perceived to be gaps in the overall argument. These ranged in date from 1957, immediately after Campbell's return from Asia, to 1983, just four years before his death.

Once I had accumulated this wonderful body of material, I was faced with an editor's greatest challenge: how to approach and assemble it.

In this regard I had three models I could follow, all provided by Joseph Campbell himself. The first was to create a truly syncretic work, taking the words from the various pieces, breaking apart the component ideas, and moving them into an order that suited the work as a whole. This model was the one followed by Campbell in assembling the posthumous works of Heinrich Zimmer. Unfortunately, I didn't feel quite the mastery of the material that Campbell himself possessed.

The second model that Campbell provided was a simple anthology—a series of articles unconnected except by theme. This was the approach that Campbell took in compiling his first omnibus essay collection, *The Flight of the Wild Gander: Explorations in the Mythological Dimension.* I felt that, with a series of lectures on so relatively focused a subject, this approach would lead to too many redundancies and too little continuity.

The last approach—the one that I finally took—was a middle road. This was the method undertaken by Campbell in preparing his popular book on personal myth, *Myths to Live By.* For that work, Campbell had taken a selection of his lecture transcripts, put them into a logical progression, and then edited them heavily in order to remove repetition, reinforce the development of ideas, and create a unified rhetorical statement.

The reader will judge how well I have succeeded. The startling connections and remarkable conclusions you find in this volume, you may ascribe to Joseph Campbell. Any gaps or logical inconsistencies you may lay at my feet.

Since I have mixed a number of lecture extracts and article fragments in with the talks that form the main body of this piece, and since I have consolidated some overlapping sections in order to avoid redundancy without losing any of Campbell's more interesting observations, I have moved and combined many passages. I hope the reader will not be surprised or disappointed, therefore, that the chapters in this book no longer serve as transcripts of the original lectures.

In terms of the voice of the piece, I have attempted to maintain Mr. Campbell's wonderful, informal speaking style. Following my predecessor, Dr. Kennedy, in his foreword to *Thou Art That,* I urge the reader, "This book is best entered as one would the hall, the classroom, or the study to find Campbell in mid-sentence, expanding as enthusiastically at eighty as he did at forty on the universe of mythology that was indeed his bliss."

I would like to acknowledge the following people for their invaluable contribution to this work: Bob Walter, president of the Joseph Campbell Foundation, for providing the vision for this series and this volume; Mark Watts, for assembling the audio; Jason Gardner, who has overseen all of the volumes of the Collected Works of Joseph Campbell series at New World Library with calm humor and insight; Tona Pearce Myers, production director, and Mary Ann Casler, art director, at New World Library, along with their valiant crew; Mike Ashby, polyglot copy editor extraordinaire; and my wife, Maura Vaughn, whose unflagging support and patience have been truly heroic.

David Kudler
March 11, 2003

"Bring me a fruit of that banyan tree."
"Here it is, venerable Sir."
"Break it."
"It is broken, venerable Sir."
"What do you see there?"
"These seeds, exceedingly small."
"Break one of these, my son."
"It is broken, venerable Sir."
"What do you see there?"
"Nothing at all, venerable Sir."
The father said: "That subtle essence, my dear, which you do not perceive there—from that very essence this great banyan arises. Believe me, my dear. Now, that which is the subtle essence—in it all that exists has its self. That is the True. That is the Self. Thou art that, Svetaketu."

—The Chhāndogya Upaniṣad, chapter 12

Jesus said, "I am the light that is over all things. I am all: from me all came forth, and to me all attained. Split a piece of wood; I am there. Lift up the stone, and you will find me there."

—The Gospel According to Saint Thomas, Logion 77

INTRODUCTION

THE HUMBLING OF INDRA[1]

Myths do not belong, properly, to the rational mind. Rather, they bubble up from deep in the wells of what Carl Jung called the collective unconscious.[2]

I think what happens in our mythology here in the West is that the mythological archetypal symbols have come to be interpreted as facts. Jesus *was* born of a virgin. Jesus *was* resurrected from the dead. Jesus *went* to heaven by ascension. Unfortunately, in our age of scientific skepticism we know these things did not actually happen, and so the mythic forms are called falsehoods. The word *myth* now means falsehood, and so we have lost the symbols and that mysterious world of which they speak. But we need the symbols, and so they come up in disturbed dreams and nightmares that are then dealt with by psychiatrists. It was Sigmund Freud, Carl Jung, and Jacob Adler who realized that the figures of dreams are really figures of personal mythologization. You create your own imagery related to the archetypes.

At present, our culture has rejected this world of symbology. It has gone into an economic and political phase, where spiritual principles are completely disregarded. You may have practical ethics and that kind of thing, but there is no spirituality in any aspect of our contemporary

Western civilization. Our religious life is ethical, not mystical. The mystery has gone and society is disintegrating as a result.

The question is whether or not there can ever be a recovery of the mythological, mystical realization of the miracle of life of which human beings are a manifestation.

We take the Old Testament God to be a fact, not a symbol. The Holy Land is a specific place and no other, man is superior to the beasts, and nature has fallen. With the Fall in the Garden of Eden, nature becomes a corrupt force, so we do not give ourselves to nature as Chief Seattle did.[3] We will correct nature. We develop ideas of good and evil in nature, and we are supposed to be on the side of the good, which creates an obvious tension. We don't yield to nature. The term *nature religions* has become the object of rejection and abuse. But what else are you going to worship? Some figment of your imagination that you have put up in the clouds? A strange thing has happened. It is so extreme that if you don't believe in a figure, you don't have any worship. Now everything is lost!

In the Puritan period we had the rejection of the whole iconography of the Christian myth and of the rituals by which it was delivered to your soul. The whole thing was rendered simply as a rational performance of bringing people of goodwill together, particularly those in that particular church. But even that has been torn apart bit by bit.

What do we read? We read newspapers concerned with wars, murders, rapes, politicians, and athletes, and that's about it. This is the reading that people used to devote to worship, to legends of deities who represent the founding figures of their lives and religion. People today are hunting around for something they have lost. Some of them know that they're hunting. The ones who don't are having a really hard time.

Now I will tell you a little story. I have only a tiny television set, the size of a postcard, which I bought many years ago when I was on TV and wanted to see myself.[4] After that I never watched it much, but when the Moon shots started, I spent day after day glued to the screen, just watching them. One of the thrilling moments for me was when the astronauts were on the way back and Houston ground control asked them, "Who is navigating now?" The reply that came back was, "Newton."

I immediately thought of Kant's "Transcendental Aesthetic," the first section of his *Critique of Pure Reason,* where he says that time and space are forms of sensibility and that they are essential to our mode of experience. We can't experience anything outside of them. They are a priori forms. So it seems we know the laws of space before we get there. In his introduction to metaphysics, Kant asks, "How is it that we can be certain that mathematical calculations made in this space here will work in that space there?"[5] The answer came to me from these men. "There is only one space because there is only one mind at work here."

Here were these chaps spinning around, hundreds of thousands of miles out in space. Enough was known of the laws of space to know just what energy should be put out of the rockets and at what angle to bring them down within a mile of a boat waiting for them in the Pacific Ocean. This was fantastic.

The knowledge of space is the knowledge of our lives. We're born from space. It was from space that the Big Bang came that sent forth galaxies, and out of the galaxies, solar systems. The planet we are on is a little pebble in one of these things, and we have grown out of the earth of this pebble. This is the fantastic mythology that's waiting for somebody to write poems about.

Mythology is composed by poets out of their insights and realizations. Mythologies are not invented; they are found. You can no more tell us what your dream is going to be tonight than we can invent a myth. Myths come from the mystical region of essential experience.

The other thing those young men said upon their return was that the Earth was like an oasis in the desert of space. The appreciation and the love for our Earth that came through in that moment rang like the words of Chief Seattle: "The Earth does not belong to Man; Man belongs to the Earth."[6]

"Let's take care of it"—I heard this theme from Apollo astronaut Rusty Schweickart, and it was, to me, a fabulous statement. He was in a module on one of those trips, and he was given what was called an EVA (Extravehicular Assignment). He was to go out of the module wearing his space suit, attached to the ship by an umbilical. Well, inside the module they had a little trouble and so he had five minutes with nothing to do. He was traveling through space at eighteen thousand miles an hour, and there was no wind and no sound and over there was the Sun and over here was the Earth and there was the Moon and this beautiful man said, "I asked myself, What have I ever done to have this experience?"

This is what is known as the sublime, the experience either of space or of energy that is so prodigious that the individual simply diminishes out of sight. I have talked with people who were in some of the German cities during the British and American saturation bombings in World War II, and they told me it was a sublime experience. So there is more than beauty in the world—there is the sublime. The mythology coming to us from space is sublime.

It is interesting that all of these mythologies that we talk about involve the Moon and the Sun. It was thought by the ancients that the Moon and the Sun were the realms of the spirit. But we know that they're made of the same stuff we're made of, and so the earlier separation of Earth and spirit doesn't work anymore. The amusing thing to me is that the mythology that really fits this worldview is Hinduism.

The Earth is the energy of which some god is a personification and of which matter is a concretization, and these things exist in eons and eons and eons of time.

Let me tell you an Indian story.

A monster named Vṛtra once managed to enclose (his name means "encloser") all the waters of the universe so that there was a great drought that lasted for thousands of years. Well, Indra, the Zeus of the Indian pantheon, finally got the idea, Why not throw a thunderbolt into this chap and blow him up? So Indra, who apparently was a slow thinker, took a thunderbolt, threw it into the midst of Vṛtra, and pow! Vṛtra blows up and the waters flow forth and the Earth and universe are refreshed.

Well then Indra thinks, "How great I am," so he goes up to the cosmic mountain, Mount Meru, the Olympus of the Indian gods, and notices that all the palaces there had fallen into decay. "Well, now I'm going to build up a whole new city here—one worthy of my dignity." He gets hold of Viśvakarman, the craftsman of the gods, and tells him his plans.

He says, "Look, let's get to work here and build up this city. I think we could have palaces here and towers there, lotus plants here, etc. etc."

So Viśvakarman starts to work, but every time Indra comes back, he has bigger and better ideas about the palace, and Viśvakarman begins to think, "My god, we're both immortal, so this thing's going to go on forever. What can I do?"

He decides to go and complain to Brahmā, the so-called creator of the phenomenal world. Brahmā is seated on a lotus (that's the way Brahmā is enthroned), and Brahmā and the lotus grow through Viṣṇu's navel. Viṣṇu is floating on the cosmic ocean, couched on a great serpent, whose name is Ananta (which means "never ending").

So here's the scene. Out in the water Viṣṇu is asleep and Brahmā is sitting on the lotus. Viśvakarman comes in and after much bowing and scraping, he says, "Listen, I'm in trouble." Then he tells his story to Brahmā, who says, "That's okay. I'll fix everything."

The next morning the porter at the gate of a palace being built notices a blue-black *brahmin* boy whose beauty has drawn a lot of children around him. The porter goes back to Indra and says, "I think it would be auspicious to invite this beautiful young *brahmin* boy into the palace and give him hospitality." Indra agrees that this would be a propitious thing to do, so the young boy is invited in. Indra is seated on his throne, and after the ceremonies of hospitality, he says, "Well young man, what brings you to the palace?"

With a voice like thunder on the horizon, the boy says, "I have heard that you are building the greatest palace that has ever been built by any Indra, and now that I have surveyed it, I can tell you that, indeed, no Indra has ever built a palace like this."

Nonplussed, Indra says, "Indras before me? What are you talking about?"

"Yes, Indras before you," says the young boy. "Just think, the lotus grows from Viṣṇu's navel, the lotus opens, and on it sits Brahmā. Brahmā opens his eyes and a universe comes into being, governed by an Indra. He closes his eyes. He opens his eyes—another universe. He closes his eyes . . . and for three hundred and sixty Brahmā years, Brahmā does this. Then the lotus withdraws, and after endless time another lotus opens, the Brahmā appears, he opens his eyes, he closes his eyes . . . Indras, Indras, Indras.

"Now, consider all the galaxies in space and outer space, each one a lotus, each one with his Brahmā. There may be wise men in your court who would volunteer to count the drops in the ocean and the grains of sand on the beaches of the world, but who would count those Brahmās, let alone Indras?"

While he's talking, there comes walking across the floor of the palace a parade of ants in perfect rows, and the boy looks at them and laughs. Indra's beard prickles; his whiskers rise; he says, "Now what? What are you laughing at?"

The boy says, "Don't ask me unless you're ready to be hurt."

Indra says, "I ask."

The boy waves his hand at the ranks of ants and says, "All former Indras. They have gone through innumerable incarnations and they have risen in the ranks of the heavens and they have all come to the high throne of Indra and killed the dragon Vṛtra. Then they all say, 'How great I am,' and down they go."

At this point a crotchety old yogi comes in who is wearing nothing but a waistband, and he has an umbrella made of banana leaves over his head. On his chest is a little circle of hairs, and the young boy looks at him and asks the very questions that are in Indra's mind. "Who are you? What's your name? Where do you live? Where's your family? Where's your home?"

"I don't have a family, I don't have a house. Life is short. This parasol is good enough for me. I just worship Viṣṇu. As for these hairs, it's curious; every time an Indra dies, one hair drops out. Half of them are gone. Pretty soon they'll all be gone. Why build a house?"

Well, these two were actually Viṣṇu and Śiva. They had come for the instruction of Indra, and once he had heard them, they left. Well, Indra is shattered, and when Bṛhaspati, the priest of the gods, comes in, Indra says, "I'm going out to be a yogi. I'm going to worship Viṣṇu's feet."

So he goes to his wife, the great queen Indrani, and he says, "Darling, I'm going to leave you. I'm going out into the forest to become a yogi. I'm going to drop all this monkey show about the kingship of the world and I'm going to worship Viṣṇu's feet."

Well, she looks at him for a while, and then she goes to Bṛhaspati and tells him what has happened. "He's got it in his head that he's going to go out and be a yogi."

So the priest takes her by the hand and they go and sit down in front of the throne of Indra, and the priest says to him, "You are on the throne of the universe. You represent virtue and duty—*dharma*—and you incarnate the divine spirit in this earthly role. I have already written a great book for you on the art of politics—how to maintain the state, how to win wars, etc. Now I am going to write a book for you on the art of love so that the other aspect of your life, with you and Indrani here, will also become a revelation of the divine spirit dwelling in us all. Anyone can become a yogi, but how about representing in the life of the world the immanence of this mystery of eternity?"

So Indra was saved from the trouble, you might say, of going out and becoming a yogi. He had it all within himself now, as we all do. All you have to do is wake up to the fact that you are a manifestation of the eternal.

This story, known as "The Humbling of Indra," appears in the Brahmavaivarta Purāṇa. The Purāṇas are Indian holy texts from around A.D. 400. The amazing thing about Indian mythology is that it could absorb the universe we talk about now, with the great cycles of stellar lives, the galaxies beyond galaxies, and the comings and goings of universes. What this does is diminish the force of the present moment.

All of our problems about atom bombs blowing up the universe, so what? There have been universes and universes before, every one of them blown up by an atom bomb. So now you identify yourself with the eternal that is within you and within all things. It doesn't mean you want to see the atom bomb come, but you don't spend your time worrying about it.

One of the great temptations of the Buddha was the temptation of lust. The other temptation was the temptation of the fear of death. This is a nice theme for meditation on the fear of death. Life throws up around us these temptations, these distractions, and the problem is to find the immovable center within. Then you can survive anything. Myth will help you do that. This doesn't mean you shouldn't go out on picket lines about atomic research. Go ahead, but do it playfully. The universe is God's play.

CHAPTER I

The Birth of Brahman

Interpreting Oriental Myth[7]

West and East

Some years ago, I had the privilege of being invited to a series of talks that Martin Buber, the Austrian-Israeli theologian, was giving at Columbia.[8] This was a very impressive man: very small, with an imposing head and an extraordinary eloquence in his speech. When one realized that English was his second language, it was actually incredible to hear the ease and fluency with which he presented these complex ideas.

As the talks went on, however, I became more and more uncertain about the meaning of a certain word he was using. The word, curiously, was *God.* I couldn't tell whether he was referring to the transcendent, mysterious source of this prodigious universe or one or another of the stages of development of the principal character in the Old Testament—or somebody with whom Martin Buber was occasionally having conversation.

He stopped in the midst of one of his talks and said, looking sad, "It pains me to speak of God in the third person." Later, when I reported this remark to Gershom Scholem, he shook his head and said, "Sometimes he does go too far."[9]

It was during the third lecture that I got up my nerve to raise my hand. Very gently and nicely he asked, "What is it, Mr. Campbell?"

"Well," I said, "there is a word being used here this evening that I just can't follow; I don't know what it refers to."

"What is that word?"

I said, "God."

Well, his eyes opened. He looked in utter amazement at me and he said, "You don't know what God means?"

I said, "I don't know what you mean by God. You're telling us that God has hidden his face. Now, I'm just back from India, where people are experiencing and beholding God all the time."[10]

"Well," he said, "do you mean to compare?..."

Unfortunately, this exchange didn't quite fit with the ecumenical spirit of the occasion, and the chairman cut in very abruptly and said, "No, Dr. Buber, Mr. Campbell just wants to know what you mean by God."

He backed away and then, acting as though it were an inconsequential matter, he said, "Everyone must come out of his exile in his own way."

Well, that might have been perfectly all right from Dr. Buber's standpoint. But what struck me immediately was that the whole point of Oriental wisdom and mythic themes is that we are *not* in exile—that the god is within you. You can't be exiled from it. All that can happen is that you can fail to know it, that you don't realize it, that you haven't found a way to open your consciousness to this presence that is right within you.

This is a very important line of differentiation between the traditions of one world—the Orient—and the other, the Occident. What are these two worlds and what line divides them? In terms of mythic and religious culture, I think you could draw the line through what we used to call Persia, sixty degrees east of Greenwich.

Eastward of that line there are two creative, high-culture centers: one is India, and the other is the Far East—China, Southeast Asia, and Japan. By high culture I mean literate civilizations with writing, monumental architecture, and so forth. Westward of that line there are likewise two creative, high-culture centers: the Near East, or Levant, which includes Egypt, and Europe.

When you consider the two eastern domains, they are isolated from each other and from everyone else. India has the Himalayas to the north and great oceans around. China likewise has the great deserts to the west and the ocean all about. New influences have therefore never come into those domains in massive force; they have come in gradually and been assimilated into the culture that was already present.

The European and Near Eastern domains, however, are in immediate and constant contact. There are very accessible arteries of transportation: the Mediterranean and Black Seas and rivers such as the Danube and others. In addition, both of these domains are wide open to massive invasion from the north and from the south.

Historically, there were two very important invading peoples. One was the northern nomadic hunting and fighting people, the Aryans, who came down into the European high-culture domain from the grass plains of northern Europe. The other, equally belligerent influence was the Semite tribes, sweeping into the river plains of the Levant from the Syro-Arabian desert.

These invasions continually disturbed the existing culture patterns. So we have in the Occident a history of disintegration and reintegration—in other words, progress. There has been terrific, continual change. Where you have a number of peoples influencing each other, there come into collision a great many contrary ideas that then must fight it out.

When one turns from the Western world—with its very complex philosophical and religious history—to the East, one gets a sense of going to a world where all of the vegetation is, let us say, palms—different kinds of palms, but all essentially alike. There are a few essential themes that run through the whole system and have been there for a long, long time.

When did the high-culture forms enter the domains of India and the Far East? Indian cultural tradition began with the Indus Valley civilization, about 2500 B.C. The culture in the Far East begins in China with the Shang dynasty, at about 1600 B.C.[11] Both of these dates lie within the Bronze Age.

Now you must remember that the whole development of the high-culture world commences in the Near East, the great realm of Mesopotamia and Egypt, starting about 8000 B.C. with the development of agriculture and animal husbandry. Before those times, as far as we know, people everywhere lived by foraging and hunting. Suddenly, we have the establishment of substantial economies and the gradual growth of quite complex societies. By about the fourth millennium B.C.—particularly in the Tigris-Euphrates valleys—you find relatively large, complicated cities: ancient Sumer, Ur, Akkad, and a whole constellation of others.

Because of the magnitude of the community, these societies developed a division of labor: there were professional governing people, professional priests, professional merchants, and professional tillers of the soil. As a result of the fact of this professionalism, astonishingly rapid advances in knowledge, skills, and crafts took place.

The knowledge that is most important to our concern is that of the priests. It is during this period—about 3500 B.C.—that the arts of writing, of mathematical calculation, of controlled astronomical observation, and also of tax collecting were invented. The idea of the king as a central coordinating factor within a differentiated society comes into being here.

One of most profound recognitions that the priests made during this period was that the planets—the seven visible spheres of the Sun, the Moon, Mercury, Venus, Mars, Jupiter, and Saturn—move at mathematically calculable rates through the fixed stars. This concept inspired a totally new notion of the universe: a cosmos of mathematically controlled cosmic regularity.

This notion rested on the idea that the cosmos is not ruled by a personal god; rather, an impersonal power moves with irresistible regularity in the courses of the rise and fall of the day and the night, the waxing and waning of the Moon, the coming and going of the year, and then, beyond that, the passing of the great year, the eon of the total round of the cosmos. This idea inspired the myths of the Bronze Age civilizations, and it is the basic idea of the Oriental philosophies to this day.

The Chinese concept of the Tao refers to a cosmic order of impersonal character, where light and dark alternate in emphasis and in influence and force, in a regular cosmic round. The Indian idea of *dharma,* too, refers to a cosmic order, as do the ancient Egyptian idea of *ma'at* and the Sumerian idea of *me.* These are all images of an impersonal cosmic order within which the deities function as bureaucrats.

The gods are not the controlling agencies—the controlling agency has no personality whatsoever. The deities administer this impersonal process; they have different departments of concern, and what they represent are personifications of the forces of nature. Those forces that are of nature, of the cosmos, are the forces also that operate within you, in your nature. So the deities that are without are also within.

This is the great idea of the hieratic society: that the social order functions to make those archetypal patterns visible in the arts, in the architecture, in the philosophy. The society itself then becomes a kind of icon, a symbolic rendering of these cosmic models.

The mythology of a people presents a grandiose poetic image, and like all poetic images, it refers past itself to principles that are mysterious and ineffable. There are four basic functions of a traditional mythology of this sort. The first must be to open the mind of everybody in the society to that mystery dimension that cannot be analyzed, cannot be talked about but can only be experienced as out there and in here at once.

The second function of a mythology is to present an image of the universe that connects the transcendent to the world of everyday experience. This cosmic image must reflect that mystery so that all the stars and little animals and trees and mountains are seen to express this unfathomable dimension.

The third function is to present a social order by which people will be coordinated to the mystery. The king, then, sits in the center as the coordinating principle of the city-state. He radiates solar light: his crown represents the light of the Sun (or of the Moon). His court moves about him in hieratic charade, as though they were planets, wearing the costumes of the cosmos and so forth. We still see this symbolism in courtly protocol.

Finally the fourth function of the mythology is to carry the individual through the course of life. It must carry the individual from the attitudes of dependency of childhood to adult responsibility (responsibility as defined in the terms of that particular culture) and then out in the way of old age and passage beyond the Dark Gate.

So that the macrocosm of the great cosmos, the microcosm of the individual, and what I sometimes call the mezzocosm—the order of the society—are all coordinated in one great unit, pointing to this mystery dimension. This is what underlies the Oriental beauty, the marvel of the Oriental cities, the Oriental philosophies, the Oriental poetry and art. When one goes there, of course, one may be physically shocked by the squalor and misery of the people and the life they're living there. Yet this coordinating principle comes shining through all the poverty in a strangely fascinating way, shining with the radiance of this mythic world. One finds also in the people themselves a very strange acquiesence to this, which, of course, exasperates social workers but delights the clergy; the people are resting well in what we call God, let us say, and they do experience this radiance through their lives.

The fundamental thought in the Oriental philosophical world is that the mysterious, ultimate truth, that which you seek to know, is absolutely beyond all definition. All categories of thought, all modes of imaging fall short of it. When we ask, "Is God merciful, just, loving? Does he love me, does he love my people more than those? Are these not chosen, are those not rejected?" this from the Oriental standpoint is sheer kindergarten stuff. This is the projection of anthropomorphic forms of thought and feeling upon a mystery that transcends even the categories of being and nonbeing. The categories of logic, the forms of sensibilities of time and space—all of these are functions of human thought, and the mystery that you're seeking lies beyond it. This is taken seriously; the absolute is absolutely transcendent of all thought.

In Occidental theology, the word *transcendent* is used to mean *outside of the world.* In the East, it means *outside of thought.* To imagine that your definitions of your God have anything to do with that ultimate mystery is a form of sheer idolatry from this standpoint. Your God is good enough for you and mine's good enough for me. A God, from this point of view, is merely a reflex of one's ability to conceive of God. Since people have various abilities of this sort, they have various powers of apprehending God.

The fundamental theological thought is that only God can know God. That's the main idea of the Trinity. In order to know the Father, one must oneself be God. In Christianity, that's the role that the Son is supposed to fill. Then, between the knower and the known there is the relationship that's represented by the Holy Ghost. Each of us is moving toward the fulfillment of the knowledge of the second person, the Christ, knowing the Father. You have exactly the same ideas in Hindu and Buddhist theology.

In the East, however, this relationship is viewed slightly differently: that which is absolutely transcendent of all knowledge is the basis of your own being. It is you; it is immanent within you. This fundamental Oriental statement appears in the Chhāndogya Upaniṣad as early as the eighth century B.C.: *Tat tvam asi,* "thou art that." You yourself are that which you would know. However, this "you" is not the you that you identify with, not this phenomenon in time and space that can be named, that can be identified, that can be described. That is not it, and so we also have the Sanskrit phrase, *Neti, neti*—"not this, not this!" Anything that you can name about yourself is not it. Therefore, when you have erased all that you can name and have broken through, then you have come to it. This is a very different sort of calculus. In this equation, a is you and x is the mystery and $a = x$—you are that mystery, but not the "you" that you think you are. The you that you think you are is not it and the you that you can't even think about *is* it. This paradox, this absurdity, is the essential mystery of the East.

Now compare that with the situation in the world of the traditions that have come out of the Near East: Judaism, Christianity, and Islam. Here, God created the world. Creator and creature are not the same, and to make that remark, "I am it," is the basic blasphemy in the West. When Christ said, "I and the Father are one," he was crucified; that was blasphemy. When the great Sufi mystic al-Hallaj said essentially the same thing nine hundred years later, he was crucified as well; that was blasphemy. But al-Hallaj revealed the secret: he said that the aim of the mystic is to be united with the divine. He is like a moth at night who sees a flame in a lamp and, wishing to unite with the flame and be one with it, batters his wings on the glass. At morning he goes back, battered, to his friends, and he says, "What an experience I had last night; what I beheld!" The next night, he manages to slip through the glass and indeed unites with the flame. That is the goal of the mystic. Who helps him to it? Those stupid orthodox people who crucify him. They become the vehicle of the mystic's fulfillment. Like al-Hallaj, Christ expressed this view when he was able to say, "Father forgive them, for they know not what they do."

So here we are, in our exile. What can we do about the mysterious, transcendent x? To find, as many a mystic has, that he was one with x and then be united with it on a martyr's pyre, this is not permitted. In our religions one can only achieve a *relationship* to x. Our religions—and this is a very important point—seek a relationship to God, not the experience of identity with the divine. How does one achieve a relationship to God? Well, there are several ways of becoming related to this particular deity. One is the way of the Jewish tradition, another is the way of the Christian, and a third is, of course, the way of Islam.

In the Jewish tradition, God has a Covenant with a certain people; no one else is in on this. How does one achieve membership in that group? This was defined in Jerusalem only a couple of years ago: by birth from a Jewish mother and by honoring the Covenant in one's life.

The Christian path to this relationship is through Jesus Christ. Christ is true God and true Man. In Christianity this is regarded as a miracle; in the East, this is the point that everybody must realize about himself. Christ through His humanity is related to us; through His divinity He relates us to God. How do we become related to Christ? By baptism into His church—again, as in Judaism, a social institution.

Islam too is a religion of relationship. In this case the relationship to Allah is through His law, the Koran, and through His prophet, Muhammad. Thus, the devout Muslim faces Mecca when he prays, not because that is where God is present but because that is where Muhammad received the holy word. *Islam* itself means "submission"; so in this youngest of the great Levantine religions, religious fulfillment is achieved through giving one's self over to this great power. Well, one does not submit to something intrinsic to oneself; one submits to the might of Allah and his law.

In the Western traditions, the faithful are utterly dependent upon social institutions—the Chosen People, the Mother Church, the Law—that have put forward pretty exorbitant claims for themselves; these claims have, in the modern era, been brought into question by certain facts that we would wish had not been found. As a result there is in the world what we call doubt and disequilibrium; this is the dilemma we face in the West.

The great thing that is happening with the recent arrival of Oriental influences into our shut-out lives is that it is waking us to our own heritage. You can recognize this experience as you read the writings of the European scholars and American Transcendentalists of the nineteenth century, who began to realize that what Buddhism and Hinduism were saying represented an awaking of their own pre-Christian hearts. They gained the recognition of what was already stated in the great Greek tradition, in the Roman tradition, and which is implicit in Celtic and Germanic mythology. These were all based on the idea of the sacred grove, the sacred object—nature within and without. In these traditions, mythology was not an account of pseudo-historical facts that are supposed to have happened somewhere else, long ago; rather, each myth is a poetic revelation of the mystery of that which is now and forever and within your own being.

I and Thou

Let me render a little myth for you. This is an old Bronze Age myth, which has come down in three separate ways through three different traditions. The first version I want to give you comes from the beginning of the Bṛhadāraṇyaka Upaniṣad, which dates from about the ninth century B.C.

In the beginning... Of course, there was no beginning, because *beginning* is a time word. As soon as you start talking about mythology, you must not take the terms concretely; that's the mistake of the whole Judeo-Christian tradition.[12] Read myths as newspaper reports by reporters who were there and it doesn't work. Reread them as poems and they become luminous.

So, in the beginning that was no beginning, there was nothing but the Self. And the Self at a moment that was no moment said, "I. *Ahaṃ. Ego.*" And as soon as it thought, "I," it experienced fear. Then it reasoned, though it wasn't very complicated reasoning—this was the very first attempt at reasoning, after all—"Since there is nothing else in the world, what do I have to be afraid of?" That eliminated the fear.

Of course, no sooner was the fear eliminated than it had desire: "I wish there were another." Well, in that state of being, a wish is as good as a fact. The Self swelled and split in half, and voilà—there were two. Each united with the other and produced something. And then she—the feminine one—said, "How can he unite with me who am of his own substance?" So she turned herself into a cow; he turned into a bull. She turned into a donkey, and he turned into a jackass. She turned into a mare, and he into a horse, and so on down to the ants. And then that which had originally said "I" looked around and said, "This world is I. I have poured it forth." So, *Ahaṃ* poured forth this universe—story number one.

From about the same date comes the second chapter of Genesis. Here we find this little chap whom God had made to tend a garden. Well, that's a dreary job, and he was lonesome. So God fashioned a lot of animals and brought them to him for his naming. Well, he could name them—what else could he do with them? God finally thought of something else; He put this lonesome mooner to sleep and drew forth what Joyce has called "the cutlet-sized consort." Then Adam looked up and he said, "Well, at last!"

Look what happened here. We have the same story of the Self splitting in two. Only this time what has split is not the deity itself but the creature of the deity. God is outside of this little event, and the whole calamity of history goes on over on our side of the footlights with Him out there, observing.

One of the great things I experienced in going to the Orient was meeting with people who had never heard of the Fall. There is no guilt with respect to some creator up there who's saying, "You ought to be this way and, instead, you are that way." This is a wonderful heart-cleansing thing. I have told many of my friends, "Save the money on psychoanalysis and go to Japan."

Now we come to our third story. The *Symposium* by Plato documents a wonderful drunken party, the greatest the world has ever seen. These Greek philosophers are sitting around, talking about love, and Aristotle relates this little myth.

It seems the original human beings had four legs and two heads; each was as big as two human beings, only—the Greeks being what they were, of course—they came in three varieties. The model on the Sun was male-male, the one on Earth was female-female, and the one on the Moon was male-female, but at any rate each was twice what each of us now is. The gods were afraid of them and so Zeus decided to cut them in half, and then Apollo pulled together their raw flesh and tied it at what is now the navel and he turned the heads around so these newly divided creatures could look at each other. Of course, what immediately happened was that all the severed couples embraced each other and refused to move. So the gods said, "Well, we won't get anything done with this kind of thing going on," so they separated the lovers far apart from each other, mixing up the different varieties and the different genders all over the place. Of course, that didn't stop our separated friends: their need to reunite with their opposites was as strong as ever. In their efforts to find each other again, they built cities and civilizations. This is really a basis for the Freudian view that all civilization is a sublimation of disappointed sex.

Here again we have the gods apart from the creatures. In this case, however, the god is not the creator of these creatures. In the Greek world a god is not our creator; rather, the gods are our big brothers, and you know how it is with big brothers: you've got to be careful with them; but they really don't have the right to order you around. Still, you'd better do what they tell you to do or else you'll get hurt. This is a quite different attitude from that of the biblical, Near Eastern tradition, where God created men to be His servants, and He gives the orders.

These then are three inflections of one old Bronze Age myth. I think this sets up very prettily the problem of these civilizations and mythologies that we're dealing with.

When you have two terms like *god* and *man,* there comes finally a question as to your ultimate loyalty: is it to God or is it to man? The recommended attitude in the Levant is submission to God, no matter what. This idea appears in Abraham's binding of Isaac, but especially in the Book of Job. In this story, God's friend for all eternity, Satan ("the enemy"), comes to him, and God says with great pride, "Have you observed My servant Job? Do you know a better man in the world? Does anyone honor Me more than he?"

Satan says, "Well, why shouldn't he? You have been good to him. Make it tough on him and see what happens."

So God says, "Okay, I'll bet you. Go ahead, do what you can." As Gilbert Murray said, this is like taking a bet that you can annoy your pet dog all you want and he won't bite.[13]

We all know what happens to the poor man: family eliminated, house burned down, cattle destroyed. He ends up on a heap of ashes with an outbreak of boils, and his friends—called Job's Comforters for some reason—come to him and say, "You must have been quite a scoundrel to have merited this." Well, he hadn't been: he got it because he was so good.

This paradox baffles certain theologians; in fact it's the point of the Book of Job.

So Job just holds out: "I didn't misbehave. I was a goodie."

Finally, he demands that God show himself, and God appears. Having put the poor man through all of this, does God say, "Job, you have been great. We had this bet, you see..."? No, none of that. Nor does He try by any roundabout way to justify what He's done. He simply says, "Are you big? Could you fill Leviathan's nose with harpoons? Try it. I did. Who are you, you little worm, even to think of understanding what's happening to you?"

At this point, Job says, "I'm ashamed of myself." He abdicates his human judgment, his human values. He pours ashes on his head and submits.

No Greek would have done that. You know what happened to the Greek gods when they were caught off base. The respect that was given them diminished. Sure, one was careful not to offend them, but more as one respects a bunch of politicians: you've got to defer to them for certain reasons—otherwise you'll end in the coop—but you don't really respect them.

At about the time that the Book of Job was being composed, Aeschylus wrote his play *Prometheus Bound;* the two works are almost exactly contemporary. Prometheus exemplifies an ideal in direct opposition to that personified by Job. He represents the affirmation of the human value system against the gods. He steals the gift of fire and delivers it to man; for doing so, he was pinned to a rock by Zeus, a great big fellow who could indeed have filled Leviathan's nose with harpoons. A little delegation comes to the titan, splayed there on the rock, with vultures daily devouring his liver, and they say, "Apologize, and he'll let you go."

Prometheus responds, "You tell him I despise him; let him do as he likes." Of course, Prometheus could take it because he was a demigod himself—and he was blessed with the ability to see into the future and know how things were going to turn out—but the attitude is that of affirmation of human values against the powers of the almighty.

Look at our modern condition: Monday, Tuesday, Wednesday, Thursday, Friday, and Saturday we are with Prometheus; then, for half an hour on the Sabbath, we are with Job. The next Monday we are on a psychiatrist's couch trying to figure out what's going on in our psyches. The answer is that we have got two totally contrary traditions that our universities and clergies have told us can somehow be coordinated—they cannot. They are as different as Europe and the Near East.

The European traditions come from the Greek, Roman, Celtic, and German worlds. These mythologies resurged in the Middle Ages in the Arthurian tradition and then in the neoclassicism of the Renaissance. The Levantine traditions come from the Old and New Testaments and the Koran, and their characteristic is authority and *islam,* which, as I have pointed out, means "submission."

Both of these are quite apart from the Eastern tradition. We usually think of Islam as somehow Oriental; it is not: it belongs to this side of that great metaphysical dividing line.

The Myth of the Lights

As I said, Bronze Age civilization moved into the Indian subcontinent about 2500 B.C. At that time, two cities suddenly appear in the Indus Valley: Mohenjo Daro and Harappa. In Europe, this is just about contemporary with the rise of the Minoan culture on Crete. These two civilizations appear at exactly the same time, and their symbols are essentially parallel. The script of the Indus has not yet been translated;[14] we don't know how to read it, but we do have a great many symbolic figures on the stamped seals that have been discovered.

Figure 1. Indus Valley Seal, c. 2000 B.C.

The first of these is the bull; this is a very important figure in the mythologies of the whole world. The horns of the bull and the horns of the Moon are equated. The Moon is that celestial sphere that dies and is resurrected. It carries its own death within it; the principle represented in the Moon is that power of life that conquers death. The bull symbolizes that lunar character, and thus, since the Moon is the sacrificial planet, the bull becomes the sacrificial animal.

Another animal that sheds death is the serpent, which sloughs its skin to be reborn, and so the serpent, like the bull, becomes a symbol linked with the Moon—a symbol of death and rebirth. The serpent is fluent and lives in waterways; it is bound to the Earth but its little flashing tongue is like a flame, so it is as though there were fire within it—the fire within water that fertilizes and fructifies and gives life.

Symbolically contrary to the Moon is the Sun, the blazing light that never dies. Wherever the Sun goes, there the light has gone. Direct experience of this light burns out life as the Sun burns out vegetation. So the interaction of these two powers—the solar power of sheer light and the lunar power of reflected light, modified to life—is one of the great mythic themes.

As the bull represents the Moon, so the lion with its solar face represents the Sun, and as the Sun pounces on the Moon as the Moon dies—

the new Moon disappears into the light of the Sun—so the lion pounces on the bull and the eagle or hawk pounces on the serpent.

These are basic mythic pairs that express two kinds of immortality. There is the immortality of the one who dies and comes back to life. That is the world of the fathers; in many cultures, the ancestors are supposed to live on the Moon. The other immortality is that of the one who has gone through the golden Sun door and will never return: he has left his body as a burned out ash on this side of the Sun; his soul has passed beyond.

The idea of the reincarnating principle is thus of two orders: first, the reincarnating principle that puts on bodies and puts them off as the Moon puts on and puts off its light body; and the other is that principle of sheer light that never dies, the light that is incarnate and immanent in all.

Now one of the aims of all of the high-culture religions on the Oriental side of the line is to *realize one's own identity with that solar light.*

Once, when I was teaching a lecture hall full of teenage boys, I was struggling to find a metaphor that would make sense of this idea. I looked up for inspiration, and there it was. I asked the boys to look up at the lights on the ceiling. Each bulb carries the light. We can think of this totality as many bulbs; this is the lunar world of multiple entities. On the other hand we can focus on the one light that emanates from all the bulbs. This is the solar consciousness. What are we focusing on, the light or the lights? Which way of looking at things is correct? If one bulb breaks, we take it out and put another in—is it the bulb that's important or is it the light? Then I said to the boys, "Now I look down here and I see all your heads like bulbs and within them is consciousness. What's important: this particular head or the consciousness that's in it?"

If we are interested in the bulb, in the head, in the phenomenon, we have the attitude of affirming the individual. In Japanese the world of individuals is called the *ji-hōkai,* or *individual universe,* and the world of the one light is called the *ri-hōkai,* or *one universe.* These are simply two different ways of talking about the same thing.[15] The goal of religions in the East is to get you to shift your focus from the phenomenal to the transcendent. So that you identify yourself not with the bulb, the head, the body, but with the consciousness, and when you have identified yourself with the consciousness, you have identified yourself with solar existence, what Kant called the noumenal world, and you were never born and you will never die.

The next stage of experience is that of no division between consciousness and the unity of the individual. These are simply two modes of viewing one mystery, and this then is called *ji-ri-muge:* "individual, universal, no division." The final great step of transcendent consciousness is *ji-ji-muge:* "individual, individual, no division." We are all riding on one *karma,* one universal path. We are all manifestations of one great being.

This is the doctrine of the so-called Flower Wreath, or *Avataṃsaka.* In the Buddhist *sūtra* of that name, the whole universe is described as a great net of gems. At each of its points of juncture, a gem reflects the light of all the others and is reflected in all the others; the accent is on what is reflected, not on the specific gem. This shift of accent is what is implicit in these mythologies of the Sun and the Moon. Look at any alchemical drawing, look at many an Oriental icon or *tanka* and you'll see in the two upper corners the Sun and the Moon of equal size: that is the moment of realizing the identity of the *ji* and the *ri* principles. And this is the central idea to all Oriental religion.

The Ever-Burning Sacrifice[16]

The Vedas

This world of the Indus Valley or Dravidian civilization flourished for about one thousand years, from about 2500 to 1500 B.C. Mohenjo Daro and Harappa were brick cities, with very elaborate sanitary arrangements, sewage systems, wells, and so forth. They were very mechanically laid out, with relatively little ornamentation. Curiously enough, when these cities were excavated in the 1920s, the archaeologists found no temples. They did, however, find an enormous bath. When one considers the role of bathing in modern Indian religious life, this bath becomes significant evidence that there is a continuity in the religious tradition of India that goes back before the Vedas, the great religious texts, which, as we will see, seem to date from around 1000 B.C.

These cities did not grow there indigenously; they were almost certainly plantations founded by settlers from the Iranian plateau for the exploitation of a land very rich in natural resources. Within these cities—and they seem to have been pretty darn materialistic—there is very little art. All that we have are a few tiny images, in contrast with the magnificent art, say, of contemporary Egypt, Mesopotamia, and Crete.

The major form of symbolic ornamentation that has been found is on the many small seals that have been discovered and that were used to provide signatures to letters and contracts.

These few little images do give us a view of the mythic world in the Indus Valley. The most conspicuous figure on these seals is the bull, the same bull that you see walking around the streets of Calcutta today, its horns wreathed in flowers. It's Nandi, Viṣṇu's companion. This is the bull that, in Egypt, is identified with Osiris, the god who dies and is resurrected. Again, it is the lunar bull, which represents that divinely appropriated energy of life that brings forth forms.

Through comparative study of these contemporaneous cultures, we come to understand that the horns of the bull were equated with the horns of the Moon. The Moon is in turn a symbol of death and resurrection, the eternal recurrence. The Moon remains the high symbol of the dead and resurrecting god. Even the Christian image of the Resurrection has elements of this symbolism inherent in it: Christ spends three days in the tomb, just as the Moon is three days dark; and the dating of Easter is always made in relation to the full Moon.[17]

The Moon can also be thought of as a cup that fills with ambrosia, is emptied, and then refilled. In the tropical world, the Sun is fierce and burning and desiccates the vegetation. The night Moon sends down the dew, the ambrosia, the *amrīta,* the drink of immortality that refreshes life. The Moon, of course, is in a constant state of emptying and refilling; you see it fill every month, and then unload its ambrosia onto the Earth and fill again.

Another symbol that occurs in the Dravidian seals is that of a tree with a kind of heart-shaped leaf. In Mesopotamia, this is called the Tree of Life. In India, it is the Bodhi tree, the tree under which the Buddha sat, which in Buddhism is called the "immovable

Figure 2. "Lord of the Tree of Life," Sumer, c. 2500 B.C.

point," that center point, that hub around which the whole ever-proceeding vortex revolves.

Finally, we have that one sign in the Indus Valley world that does not appear in the West, and that is a seated yogi, surrounded by animals, who bears such a striking resemblance to Śiva.

Figure 3. "Lord of the Animals," Indus Valley civilization, c. 2000 B.C.

He wears a large headdress with two horns and something coming up in between to make a three-pronged design. And he has three faces. This is the first example we have of the seated yogi: there is nothing of the sort in Sumer or Egypt in this pattern of the contemplative yogi, and so it is undoubtedly an Indian motif.

Also found were a number of magnificently rendered small images—one in bronze and others in stone—of dancers: one a male dancer in a posture that again suggests that of the dancing Śiva (except, of course, that there are only two arms instead of four); another a dancing girl—a very handsome little bronze of a very lean girl with heavy bracelets on, standing in a rather rakish posture that suggests the *devadāsī,* or dancing priestess. We know that in ancient Mesopotamia there were cults in which dancing priestesses played an important role. Here is considerable evidence for a continuity of tradition between the three culture worlds of Egypt, Mesopotamia, and India, but also for a specific definition of the Indian—and there is much evidence for that in the finds of the Indus Valley.

This very early Dravidian culture is actually associated with yoga, then, in some form.

Then, around 1500 B.C., the Vedic Aryans came sweeping in from the north. These were cousins of the Dorian and Achaean Greeks that we know from Homer; this invasion is exactly contemporary with the Greeks coming into Crete and overcoming that civilization.

If you read the Homeric epics, you will have a very good picture of the Aryan style. These were a nomadic warrior people. The earlier Dravidians were city people, trading people, agriculturalists. In contrast, the Aryans' principal economic resource was their herds and flocks. It seems that it was the Aryans who brought in the *brahmins*—the magician-priest class—and the *kṣatriya,* or warrior class. These two go together. They represent the conquering tradition. So we have a two-tier social system: the Aryan *brahmins* and *kṣatriya* on the top, the native merchants (*vaiśya*) and peasants (*śūdra*) on the bottom. This starts a tension in the Indian world that is quite new. A long period of interaction between these two worlds now follows.

The principal evidence we have for Aryan thought in India is a series of hymns addressed to the Indian gods: the celebrated Vedas. (The Indians themselves like to speak of the Vedas as being ten thousand, twenty thousand years old, but nothing of the kind can be established. They are comparatively late in the perspective of world history.) *Veda* means "knowledge," the manifestations of the knowledge of divine truth.

You know that the Greeks had sacrificial rites. They would erect an altar and burn holocausts upon it, sharing the meat of the slaughtered animals with the gods. The same scene is set in the Vedic sacrifice. When you are a settled people, you can worship or revere the divinity of this stone, this tree, this pond. When you are a nomadic people, you revere what is everywhere: the great sky and its light, the blowing clouds and the winds, the broad Earth or the fire of your altar of sacrifice. The *brahmins,* who were the magicians or priests of these warriors, like Calchas in *The Iliad,* would build their altars anywhere; they would be symbolically constructed so as to imitate the form of the cosmos. The priests would come pouring libations into the flames, the flame being a god, Agni, who as the mouth of the deities would consume the sacrifice and give it to the gods. The priests would invoke the deities to participate in the sacrifice. The hymns that were sung were, in fact, the Vedas, the sacred texts—the prayers that were heard, so to say, from the song of the universe.

So, an altar would be built and the hymns of the priests would conjure the gods to the rite. Then the gods would be praised and the meal shared with them. Next comes this wonderful idea that moves the Aryans completely into an Indian mode of thought—the Greeks never had this idea—since through our sacrifice we can influence the gods, *we and our sacrifice are stronger than the gods.* There are two kinds of gods: there are the gods such as Indra and his lot, and then there are the *brahmins.* If you ask which is the stronger, the answer is the *brahmins.* That put the priests on the top of the universe; indeed, that put the human being on the top of the universe. There is not a power in the world greater than a fulfilled, noble human being.

> Hearken men, my brothers:
> Man is the truth above all truths;
> There is nothing above that![18]

This is what thrilled Schopenhauer and the other Western philosophers of the nineteenth century when they read it.

So, once these Aryan priests realized that, if their sacrifice could bring the gods to them, the sacrifice was stronger than the gods, there comes an emphasis on the sacrifice. The act of the sacrifice—the lighting of the fire and the magic of the sacrifice—was a tremendously important act. And the details of the sacrifice were correlated with the details of the cosmos and the details of the psyche: there was a threefold allegory built. The Sun is the counterpart of the eye and the eye is the counterpart of the fire—that sort of thing. The wind is the counterpart of the breath, and the breeze that blows into the fire is the counterpart of the breath, etc. And so here are all these allegories suggesting a correspondence of microcosm, macrocosm, and sacrifice, with the sacrifice itself as the central symbol and central point of concentration.

The energy in that sacrifice was called *Brahman.*

The Face of Glory

So as far as we can see now, if we interpret the process in an evolutionary way, the idea of the *Brahman* seems to have occurred first in relationship to a sacrifice. The manipulation of the instruments of the sacrifice was a magical process of transformation, and a set of texts minutely describes how this is to be achieved. The *Brahmanas,* as they are known, interpret the Vedas in this way. These elaborate theological prose texts serve as a set of stage directions, as it were, to the sacred hymns.

The *kṣatriya* kings of the period patronized the Brahmanical *brahmin* priests and their sacrifices. The sacrifices themselves were extremely elaborate affairs, involving many priests, chanting long and difficult hymns, learned by heart. The slightest mistake or even slip of pronunciation would destroy the effect of the whole thing and all would have to start again. This involved an extraordinarily elaborate activity, which required royal support.

But then came the heretical movement of the so-called forest philosophers. Somewhere about the eighth century B.C., they seem to have come up with the idea that *Brahman,* that energy which is the energy of the sacrifice, is the energy also of all life.

The great texts of this movement are the Upaniṣads, the Platonic dialogues of the Indian tradition. They are profoundly thought-through investigations of the ultimate power. Is the ultimate power that of the Sun? That of the sacrifice? That of the mind? Is it that of the feelings? Finally it is found that the energy that inhabits life is the same as that which lives in the sacrifice, in the Sun, and in all—and one can seek it here.

This, in a way, threatened to render invalid all of the sacrifices and their activities. In the classical world of the Greeks, the philosophers broke away from the religious traditions. But in India, the two stayed together. There is a very interesting interplay from here on between the two, a mutual fructification, back and forth.

There is a question as to what the influence was that brought this transformation about, this shift from the Aryan sacrifice to contemplation. The answer seems to be that a resurgence of the earlier tradition, that of Mohenjo Daro and the Dravidian times, as illustrated by the seated yogic figure from the seal. There is good reason to believe that, after the Aryans had been some eight hundred years in India, their political power was beginning to lose its force, and through intermarriage and a renaissance of the earlier tradition, the mixing of the two culture worlds took place. Indian thinking from here on is a mixture of these two worlds, the Aryan and the Dravidian.

Now comes the problem of what, in all this tradition, belongs to the Dravidian and what to the Aryan inheritance. We know that the Aryans—when we think of the Greeks—had no such world-renouncing attitude as that which distinguishes, for instance, early Buddhism, Hinduism, or Jainism. Their attitude is rather that of a vigorous, aggressive world affirmation. What they wanted was health, long life, flocks, and children. The seated yogi figure of the Indus Valley seal would seem to suggest that the whole pattern of yogic contemplation belongs rather to the earlier tradition.

Where does this world negation come from? We must look back to the whole idea of sacrifice. Since the sacrifice is the secret of the universe, what is the nature of the sacrifice? The nature of the sacrifice is that a sacrificial offering is poured into a fire; that sacrificial offering is a symbol of God—indeed, it is itself a god. It's called *soma.* It is an intoxicating liquid like the wine of the Greeks. Like wine, *soma* is pressed from a plant. That plant is refreshed by the dew of the Moon. The Moon is the celestial bull. It is as though you had the divine procreating energy of the bull caught here and were pouring it into the fire. Next, when you take food to your mouth and eat it, the fire in you consumes that food just as Agni consumed *soma;* therefore eating food is a sacrifice.

The two consumptions—of flame feeding on the sacrifice, or of life feeding on life—are just the same. And then you die, and you are thrown to the flames, either the flames of the funeral pyre or the flames in the bellies of the worms, the vultures, or the hyenas. And you who were Agni now become *soma.* Agni, the fire, is of course also a god. Now we come to this Dionysian realization: the whole universe is an ever-burning sacrifice, unquenchable, inexhaustible, going on and on.

Once one has had this realization, there are two directions one can take: one can either say yes to the horror of this world or say no to it. If you're going to say yes, you affirm the world as it is. If you choose to say no, you turn your back on it. The concept of an originally good creation followed by a fall and then a gradual restoration, which came into our biblical tradition from Persia, does not exist here in the Orient: in this game, you have got to take it or leave it.

There is a story about Śiva. One day, he was approached by a monster, and this monster said to Śiva, "I want your consort as my mistress."

This is a bit of impudence. This is consciousness taking the role of the self. So Śiva, in his indignation, simply opened the third eye, the eye of transcendent consciousness, and a thunderbolt hit the Earth—*bang!* Dust was flying all over the place, and when it had cleared there was a ravenous, starving monster there who had been created to eat the first.

Well, the first monster is now in a surprisingly unpleasant situation. And when you are in a situation like that, the best thing to do is to throw yourself on a god's mercy. So the first monster throws himself on Śiva's mercy. Now, there are rules in this god game. When someone throws himself on your mercy, you have to grant mercy.

So Śiva said to the first, "I'll grant you mercy." To the second monster he said, "Don't eat him."

"Well," said the second monster, "I'm hungry. And I don't see anything else around here."

Śiva said, "I do. I see you yourself. Why don't you eat yourself?"

So the monster starts eating at his own feet, comes chopping up the line, and finally there is nothing left but the upper part of his face—not even the lower jaw. Well, that's a perfect image of the nature of life, the nature of which is to eat itself. This is the image of the ferocity of life. And when Śiva had seen this, he was simply charmed. He said, "You are wonderful. I will call you Face of Glory, *Kirtimukha,* and you will be placed over my shrines. And no one who does not say 'Yea' to you is worthy to come to me." And, indeed, you see this symbol placed over the entrances to Śiva's shrines. You see this same figure used in Buddhist shrines to represent the whole realm of the world and its consumption of itself. That gate is the portal to transcendence.

This is absolute affirmation of the world as it is. And the problem is to put yourself into accord with the world not as it ought to be but as it is.

This concept, that of out of the death and burning comes life, is a basic notion that underlies the great sacrificial rites in the Indian tradition. If we follow that logic one step more now—and the Indians always carry it a step

Figure 4. Stele with Kirtimukha above, c. twelfth century A.D.

further—we arrive at this thought: since that fire is within you, why bother with the *brahmins?* Come into the forest, sit down, and seek it in yourself. So we have the forest philosophers.

And here comes then the great period of the Upaniṣads, which I believe can be safely said to be the most sublime religious writings in the world. They date from about the eighth century B.C. on. What has happened? The Dravidian idea of the yogi, which did not exist with the Aryans coming in, has now combined with the Aryan tradition. There has taken place an interaction between the two peoples, and a very deep new problem comes along. How do we coordinate these two ideals—the ideal of virtue, the ideal of the society, the ideal of work for the world, what we know as *dharma,* on the one hand, and this idea of yoga on the other?

The date for the Buddha, 563 to 483 B.C., can be taken as the date of the climax and crisis of this conflict. The Buddha was not a *brahmin;* he was of the *kṣatriya* caste, the warrior lords. And in the Upaniṣads themselves, we have texts that date from this time that explore this conflict. The earliest Upaniṣads show that the original *brahmins* never knew anything about this. They got the doctrine from great kings.

Here's a short story that illustrates this. One *brahmin* goes to teach a king, and the king says to him "Teach." Then the *brahmin* begins teaching him, and the king says, "Oh I know all that, I know all that, I know all that."

Finally the king shows him a man asleep, and he speaks to the man asleep and the man doesn't answer. Then the king kicks the man and he wakes up. And the king says to the *brahmin,* "Where was that man's understanding when he was asleep?"

So you get the doctrine of life-as-dream that gets explored—as we will see—in the sacred syllable *aum.* It is from the natives of the land who were there before the Aryans came that these doctrines that we now revere as India's great doctrines really stem.

CHAPTER II

THE JĪVA'S JOURNEY

THE MYSTICAL TRADITION IN INDIA[19]

Rājā Yoga: The Serpent of the Cakras

The fundamental mystical tradition that developed in India during the upanishadic period has appeared in modified form in Buddhism, Jainism, and, of course, Hinduism. This idea has been carried into Southeast Asia, China, and Japan, where it has been inflected this way and that in terms of local circumstance and needs. If one takes the chronicles of the great Buddhist king Aśoka seriously, one can even trace connections to the neo-Platonic mysticism of the Hellenistic age and early gnostic forms of Christianity in the West.[20] But the basic tradition of Oriental mysticism is that of yoga.

The word *yoga* is from the Sanskrit root *yuj,* which means "to yoke." In yoga, we attempt to yoke our consciousness to the source of consciousness—at least that is the theory. In this view, each of us is an instrument, you might say, of consciousness, just as every bulb in that lecture hall was an instrument of electricity. Each bulb is a vehicle through which the electricity operates; so each of us is a vehicle through which consciousness operates. Not only is each of us such an instrument, but so is every animal—and even trees and crystals.

There is consciousness there; there is sensitivity there. You can see plants turn toward the Sun: that is, in Indian terms, a manifestation of consciousness.

How does one put one's mind into identity, into a state of identity, with this consciousness? There is a classical work called the Yoga Sūtras. The Sanskrit word *sūtra* is related to our word *suture,* the filament with which a doctor sews you up, a thread. *The Threads of Yoga*—it's the guiding thread to this mysterious art. The first aphorism stated in the *sūtras* is as follows: yoga is the intentional stopping of the spontaneous activity of the mind substance.

Within what is called the gross matter of the mind, there functions what we now call electricity. In the Indian tradition, this is called subtle matter—energy as form—which is seen to be in continuous activity. The goal of yoga is to make it stop being active.

The notion is that this substance takes the forms of the things that we see. The reason we see each other is that something in our mind takes the form of what's out there—an internal model of perceived reality. The difficulty is that you can't stop it from changing. Try to fix your mind for one minute on a single image or a single thought. You can look at your watch and say, "Now, I'm just going to hold one thought till the second hand swings around." You'll realize almost immediately that you are having associated thoughts; your mind is in movement. These thoughts are relevant, perhaps, but they're not one thought. It's not one thing.

What is the point in making the mind stand still? The image that is used in analogy is that of a pond with the water rippled by a wind. When the wind ripples the water, you see only broken images. Still the water and then you will see in perfect form the image that was broken up—the clouds, the trees round about. You will see also down into what is below the surface of the pond. Suddenly you see the true form that was broken up in all those moving shimmers.

The notion is that you yourself are identical with that form of forms, *Brahman,* but you identify yourself wrongly with the broken images that flicker on the surface. Just think: there are those wonderful forms there; here are these reflections always changing, and you identify yourself with the reflection instead of with the true, underlying form. As the wave ripples along, you think, Oh, here I come; oh, there I go. Yet all the time you are the substantial thing that is being reflected here in broken image.

So, when we engage in yoga, we are trying to make the pond stand still. During the later medieval period in India that is known as the Gupta period, which dates from the fourth to the sixth centuries A.D., a great system of what is known as *rājā,* or kingly, yoga developed that visualizes the idea of the energy of the spirit as a coiled serpent. This is, by analogy, a feminine serpent named the *kuṇḍalinī,* which means "the coiled-up one." It is thought of as being coiled up at the base of the spine, in the bones of the coccyx, the tailbone. The idea is that we spend most of our lives in a kind of spiritual slumber, with the *kuṇḍalinī* coiled up at the base of our spines, lacking the animation of this spiritual power. The goal of this yoga is to bring this serpent power up the spine to the head so that our whole being will be animated by the serpent power, so that our psyche is drawn up to full flowering.[21]

The spine is pictured as a tree with seven centers called wheels, *cakras.* These wheels are at certain specific points on the spinal course, often corresponding to the major endocrine glands. The first of these *cakras*—they're also called *padmās,* or lotuses—is at the base of the spine, and here is where our little serpent power is centered to begin with.

Sitting in an erect posture, thinking certain assigned thoughts, and pronouncing certain syllables, the yogi is to breathe in a certain way, inhaling through one nostril for a certain number of counts, holding, and then exhaling through the other nostril. This is an extremely challenging physical exercise as well as a spiritual one; one is to awaken this coiled-up serpent from its resting place in the base of the spine so that the head lifts and the serpent starts up the channel of the spine.

In the nineteenth century there was a marvelous Indian saint named Ramakrishna. He was quite a virtuoso at bringing this *kuṇḍalinī* power up the spine, and his disciples would say, "Oh, master, what is it like when the *kuṇḍalinī* comes up the spine?"

"Well," he'd say, "sometimes it's like an ant crawling up, sometimes it's like a mouse running up, sometimes it's like a monkey jumping from one lotus to another on the way up."

Then they'd say, "Oh, master, what is it like at this lotus, and at that, and at that and that?" He'd keep a running commentary going up through the lower *cakras,* but when he'd get up above the level of the throat, he'd pass out in a trance.

Figure 5. The path of the *kuṇḍalinī*

This is no remote, abstract subject. I have become very much interested recently in some of the researches that have been going on in relation to schizophrenia and psychosis, when people lose their grip on the conscious world, on their ego consciousness that holds them to the conscious world, and slip into the abyss of the psyche. It fascinated me long, long ago to realize how close yoga experiences were to those described by Freud, Adler, and Jung in their discussions of the deeper regions of the psyche into which people fall. There has been a great deal written about these matters in recent years by psychiatrists who very often know nothing about yoga. Yet the reports that they are writing and which one can read in the journals of the imagery of the experiences of these psychotic patients of theirs correspond point for point with the experiences of yoga.

I had a rather elaborate discussion once with an important and highly respected psychiatrist on this subject of mysticism, yoga, and psychosis, and his point if I understand correctly was that the two are just about the same, that the yogi is somehow experiencing a psychotic breakup but is not drowned in this subconscious sea that swamps the ordinary psychotic. What we are describing when we describe psychosis and the yogic experiences is the same sea, the same ocean, the same crises. The psychotic is drowning in these waters, while the yogi is swimming—and there is a difference between drowning and swimming.

So what I am going to be describing to you are these waters—or this wilderness, if you prefer that image. One day, some of your friends or perhaps you yourself may traverse this geography—by design or by psychological circumstance. So this is something not of remote exotic interest only but of a quite close concern to us all because, as the British psychiatrist Laing has said in that interesting book of his, *The Politics of Experience,* one out of ten people born in this period of ours is going to experience a psychological breakdown.[22] Likewise, Jung declares that for every lunatic in the mental wards, there are ten walking around on the street. So I would say that the odds are that I am addressing myself to at least one member of the present readership.

Here, then, is the map, as it were, the geography of the road from here to the other side and back.

Unlike Ramakrishna, I haven't been up there, so I'm going to be able to report on the upper regions there without passing out. Of course, I'll be working from reports, but I will attempt to give an idea of the full journey of the *kuṇḍalinī.*

The first lotus is called *mūlādhāra,* which means "root base." At this lotus, the serpent is coiled up and inert in its lair at the base of the spine. At this point the serpent is like a dragon. We all know the character of dragons—at least, Western dragons: they live in caves, and they have a gold hoard in the cave, and they have a beautiful girl whom they have captured in the cave. They can't do anything with either treasure or maiden, but they simply want *to hold on.* Dragons, like people whose lives are centered around the first *cakra,* are based around gripping, holding on to power, holding on to a life that is no life at all because there is no animation in it, no joy in it, no vitality in it, but just grim, dogged existence. The nature of the *kuṇḍalinī* at *mūlādhāra* is that of Ebenezer Scrooge before he undergoes that grand journey and transformation at the hands of the three ghosts in

Charles Dickens's *A Christmas Carol.* I hope you don't know anybody who lives on that level, but I do.

The aim of the yogi is to encourage the *kuṇḍalinī* to rise from its lair at the base of the spine to unite with the lord of the world, who is waiting at the crown of the head in the seventh *cakra, sahasrāra.*

"Wake, Mother!" runs a pious Bengali song:

> Wake, Mother, Wake!
>   How long hast thou been asleep
>   In the lotus of the *mūlādhāra!*
> Fulfill thy secret function:
>   Rise to the *sahasrāra,*
>   Where mighty Śiva dwells!
> Swiftly pierce the six lotuses,
>   O thou Essence of Consciousness,
>   And take away my grief![23]

An awakened *kuṇḍalinī* now starts up through the channel of the spine, the *suśumnā.*

The second *cakra* is at the level of the genitalia and is called *svādhishṭhāna,* which means "her favorite resort." This is the *cakra* that centers itself entirely around the experience of pleasure, or *kāma.* When one's spiritual energy is operating on this level, one's psychology is completely Freudian. Sex is the only aim; sex is the great frustration.

When the *kuṇḍalinī* moves up again, it reaches the level of the navel or stomach. This *cakra* is called *maṇipūra,* which means "the city of the shining jewel." Here the interest is in consuming everything, being master of everything, eating everything, turning it into your own substance; this is, after all, the *cakra* of the belly. When the energy is at this level, one's psychology is completely Nietzschean or Adlerian. One wants to consume and gain power for oneself over everything; one is driven by a will to power. This is the level at which the *artha* principle, the drive to succeed, is centered.

Most people operate on the second or third level, the pleasure or power principles. In general, Freudian psychology is based on the idea that the sex urge is the primary urge in life. The psychology of Jacob Adler is based on the idea that the will to power is the primary urge in life and all other urges are sublimations or inflections of this. The Indians say this too; they say both of these—*kāma* and *artha*—are primary urges. These are both inflections of that still deeper, dragonish will simply to be alive, but on these two higher levels, at the second and third lotuses, there is a vitality, an activity, a joy and pain in life. People on these levels are outward directed. Their individual satisfaction must come from a relationship to something outside, to an outer object. In the first case, in the case of the second *cakra,* with an erotic emphasis; in the third *cakra,* the emphasis is on conquest and defeat, whether military, financial, or erotic. Jung referred to such people as *extroverted,* turned outward.

We have already traveled through the *cakras* at which most of our lives are lived; however, we still have four levels to go.

Next comes the very interesting fourth level, at the level of the heart. You know the Roman Catholic figure of Jesus with his heart exposed, the Sacré Coeur. It is at the level of the heart that one comes first into relationship to the higher principles, of the powers of art and the spirit, which are not those of the empirical, outside environment. Once the *kuṇḍalinī* rises to this level, as Wordsworth says, one gains

> A sense sublime
> Of something far more deeply interfused,
> Whose dwelling is the light of setting suns,
> And the round ocean and the living air,
> And the blue sky, and in the mind of man.[24]

One is moved to seek that that is. It is said that the divinity meets the devotee at the level of the heart. That is to say that the divinity is coming down and the devotee reaching up. The standard symbol for this is two equilateral triangles, one atop the other. In the West, we call this the Star of David. Another image that one frequently sees in Oriental iconography is of two footprints. Those are the footprints of the divinity. Perhaps you have seen images of the Buddha's footprints, which have the symbol of the *dharmacakra,* "the wheel of law," engraved in the middle of the foot. You can go to Jerusalem and see the place where Muhammad left his footprints on the rock from which he ascended to heaven; it is around this rock that the great Al-Aqsa mosque was built. There are even little towns in India called "the footprint of Viṣṇu," where Viṣṇu came down and left his footprint. So the divinity comes down to the level of the heart: there his footprint is placed. The devotee touches the feet with the hands; one of the greetings to a sage or a monk in India is to take the dust from his feet with your hand. The hand, too, appears in many primitive shrines. In the Paleolithic ordination caves, going back as early as 30,000 B.C., one finds handprints of the devotee who touches the realm of the divinity.

Figure 6. The feet of the Buddha, c. first century B.C.

The name of the heart *cakra* is very interesting: it is called *anāhata,* which means "not hit." The full translation of its sense is this: the sound that is not made by two things striking together. Perhaps you have heard that Japanese Zen koan, "What is the sound of one hand clapping?" Well, this is it: the sound that is not made by two things striking together. Every sound that we hear is made by two things striking together: the sound of my voice is made by the wind striking the vocal cords, the sound of the violin is made by the bow rubbing on the string, the sound of a wave is made by the water splashing against the beach, and so it goes. What would the sound be that is not made by two things striking together? It is the sound of *Brahman,* the energy of which the world itself is a precipitation. As Einstein has told us, energy and mass are the same. The mass is a projection, so to say, of energy in space, or, if you will, a precipitation of energy into matter. The sound of that energy before it becomes mass is the sound that is not made by two things striking together. To get a notion of what the sound is, the Indians simply cover their ears. Try it yourself, and you can hear it. Actually, we know that this sound, too, is made by two things striking together—namely the blood swirling through the capillaries around your eardrum—but if you didn't know that you might indeed think that was the sound.

That sound is *aum.* You have probably heard the sacred syllable *aum,* and this is it, this is the sound that is not made by two things striking together. The sound "o" in Sanskrit is analyzed into two sounds: "a" and "u." This is what is known as a diphthong. So this word can be written either *om* or *aum,* and you will see it both ways. When one pronounces *aum,* the sound starts in the back of the mouth ("a") and then it fills the mouth cavity ("u") and then it closes at the lips ("m"). If this is pronounced correctly—and it's not an easy thing to do—the notion is that you have pronounced all the open sounds that a human mouth can form. Consonants are simply interruptions of these vowel sounds according to this view. So that all words and their meanings are simply broken inflections of *aum,* just as all the scattered reflections on that pond that I mentioned are merely broken inflections of that great cosmic image.

Aum is God. *Aum* is God as sound. We usually think of the divine as a form, as an image that we can visualize, but this is the sound aspect of the form that we are going to find when we meet God. It is the sound of God, the sound of the Lord of the World, out of whose thoughts, out of whose being, out of whose energy substance the world is a precipitation. *Aum* is the word of words, that original *Logos* that we find in the Gospel According to John: "In the beginning was the word, . . . and the word was God."[25]

Since *aum* is the Lord of the World, everything in the world and all the aspects of the world must be somehow understood to be included in *aum.* To understand it this way, we have to say some things in an allegorical way. "A," that fine open sound, is associated with waking consciousness, the way we experience things when we are awake. Now, when we are awake the objects that we see are not ourselves, that is to say subject of knowledge and object of knowledge are different from each other. In waking consciousness, Aristotelian logic prevails, *a* is not *b,* I am not what I see. Also, the objects that we see are what are considered to be made of gross matter; they are made of heavy substance. They are not self-luminous; rather, they must be illuminated from without.

"U" is associated with dream consciousness; now this is quite a different realm of awareness altogether. In dream, you are the subject of knowledge—you see the dream—but you are also the object of knowledge; it is your substance that embodies the dream. Though subject and object seem to be different from each other on this stage, they're not. At this point

Aristotelian logic does not work: the subject and object are the same. Furthermore, the objects are subtle objects; they can change form rapidly and effortlessly. Also, they are self-luminous: you don't have to turn a light on to see the objects in your dream.

The "m" is associated with dreamless, deep sleep. This is the realm of mystery. Consciousness is there, as potential, because the person asleep is conscious but unconscious. We know—as the king demonstrated to the *brahmin* in that upanishadic anecdote—that if we woke him there would be consciousness there, it is waiting to come forth again and it will come forth through either of these two zones, dream and waking, but at this point it is covered with darkness. Now, let us think about that consciousness which is unconscious. It is conscious of nothing. That is to say, it is not specific. It is not consciousness *in relation* to any object, either dream object or waking object.

What is the fourth syllable in the three-syllable word *aum?* It is the silence that is before and after *aum* is pronounced. That is the totality of the word and of the world now: you have the silence—that is to say non-being—and *aum,* which is being. Neither exists without the other. They are mutually interrelated. So this word when thought about contains in itself all the mysteries of the world.

However, when you say *aum,* the sound you produce is made by two things striking together, so it is not itself the sound that's not made by two things striking together. Yet by pronouncing *aum,* by repeating it, you may move your mind toward the point where it will hear the sound that is not made by two things striking together. Once you have heard that sound, you will hear it in all things. Listen to the sound of the city, listen to the sound of the icebox, listen to any sounds without personifying them and defining them and you will hear *aum.* When *aum* has been heard, since it is the very sound of your own heart and being, it will enchant you; you will be stilled by it, and you will hear it everywhere. So there is no need to look anywhere anymore. What you seek is here, to be heard within all things. The realization of this vibration occurs at the level of the *cakra* of the heart.

Once the sound *aum* has been heard, one is removed from the call of the lower drives and carried toward the heights, as it were, reaching into the void. One's nature up here is beyond description. This is the ultimate ground of one's self, the *ātman.* It is identical with the *Brahman.* One reads references to *Brahman-ātman* or *ātman-Brahman.* The two are one.

In this world of duality, *ātman* gets distilled inward into the unit known as the *jīva,* the individual soul on the inside, while the power outside toward which the soul aims itself is our old friend *Brahman.*

From this point on in the ascent of the *kuṇḍalinī,* the zeal is to cleanse one's consciousness of the interference of the phenomenal world and come to a direct confrontation with that sound, and with the image that is in accord with it. The fifth *cakra* then, at the level of the larynx, is called *viśuddha,* "the purgatorial, or cleansing, one." Here one is trying to eliminate the interposition of the world between oneself and the pure *aum,* or the world between oneself and the divine being of God. This is the *cakra* of ascetic, monkish disciplines. Those who reach this level focus their energy into religious zeal, turning that drive that was central in the third *cakra* to work on one's self, conquering one's outward-going tendencies, turning all inward, concentrating inward. *Viśuddha* correlates exactly to our concept of purgation; the passage through this *cakra* is like Purgatory, in which one purges oneself of earthly limitations in order to experience the ultimate.

This brings one next to the sixth *cakra*—*ājñā,* "the third eye." This eye of inner sight perceives the ultimate vision of the Lord of the World, that human form of the divine that transcends the human. Here the divine being is made manifest, so to say, in one's own image. And at this point, *jīva*—the soul, the individual incarnation of *Brahman* that returns to its source and is incarnated again and again—beholds the Lord, *Īśvara,* and this is what, in our Western terminology, we call *heaven.* The soul has found its proper love, and so the erotic zeal of the second *cakra,* between the legs, has found its true goal in the sixth *cakra,* between the eyes.

For the modern Western reader it will perhaps be a bit disconcerting to find that between the two ways of the yogic solitary and the so-called lover there is finally very little to choose, since the apparent form of the world is burnt to ash and left behind either way. Indeed, the goal of the two yogas is ultimately much the same; the only pertinent question from the point of view of the classical Orient is whether what is won, this way or that, is actually that permanent state of realization from which all temporality rolls away, as the waves from the leaves and the petals of a lotus.

Here, within this body, are the Ganges and the Jumna;
    Here Prayag and Benares;
    Here the Sun and Moon.
Here, within this body, are all the sacred places:
    The seats of the gods and their approaches.
I have not seen a place of pilgrimage,
    Or an abode of bliss,
Comparable to my body.[26]

The two spinal nerves at either side of the *suśumnā,* left and right, are, respectively, the channels of the female and the male energies, which the ordered breathing of the yogi is to bring together. Moreover, the *kuṇḍalinī* itself, the coiled serpent power, is conceived as female. Indeed, throughout the broad and colorful domain of Hindu myth and iconography, energy in play (kinetic energy) is conceived and represented as female, so that the word *śakti,* meaning "energy, power, capacity, strength," connotes also the goddess-consort of a god, the wife as spiritual consort of the male, and the female organ, the *yoni,* in relation to the *liṅgam.* The *kuṇḍalinī* in the *mūlādhāra* is the *śakti* of the god who dwells in the lotus at the crown of the head, with whom she is to be joined. Her voyage up the spine, therefore, is the flight of an awakened girl burning with desire *(kāma)* through a forest of perils and deceptive allures to her own extinction in fulfillment and fulfillment in extinction: a lover's quest.

Comparably, the body of perfection is androgyne—neither wholly male nor wholly female but combining both. It is represented in certain works of Hindu art as Śiva Ardhanārī, Śiva "the half *(ardha)* woman *(nārī),*" of whom the left side is female and the right male (see Figure 4). The yogi is to realize within himself this ideal through an awakening of the power *(śakti)* of his own omniscience, defending it from loss in the forest of allure and guiding it up the way to the deity of the head, who, without it, must remain, as it were, a corpse *(śāva),* dissociated from the energy of life. The male principle is represented—perhaps on the model of Indian life—as the one who would be left alone, the one who would like to be still. But the woman whispers to him of the worlds that they might bring into being, and "the corpse," Śāva, becomes Śiva, "the propitious." Śiva-Śakti, then, is the image of the perfect consciousness-in-action of the living world.

But there is another, more obvious and natural way of achieving the Śiva-Śakti union, and that is by way of the sexual act itself: and here one need not think of the analogy of god and goddess since the man and woman themselves supply both the image and the experience. Indeed, throughout the culminating period of Indian art and civilization, this way of sexual, or Tantric, yoga was held by many to be not only the most natural and easy path but also the most effective. Since hunger and sex, it was claimed, are the fundamental urges of the whole of nature, suppressing them is unnatural and continually suppressing them leads only to a state that is rather morbid than sublime. Unnatural strains should not be imposed for the realization of truth, but on the contrary, the path should be followed along which nature itself is pointing. The natural powers should not be annihilated but amplified, whereupon they will become, of themselves, transformed and yield the revelation of the Other Shore.[27]

The masculinity of the right side of the body is preponderant in the man; the femininity of the left, in the woman: and the rapture of their union—even on the lowest level of its great and soaring scale—is, therefore, a mode and signal of the "Great Delight" *(mahāsukha)*, which is the rapture and nature of Being itself.

Extreme followers of this way, the so-called Sahajayas, have no gods or god other than man, who, in the strength of his love, is divine.[28]

Nonetheless, at this level in the ascent of the *kuṇḍalinī,* the soul and its beloved, the Lord, are still two. They are distinct.

At the sixth *cakra,* everything is relationship—relationship of *I* to *thee,* of the soul to the beloved. Here we behold the divine aim of all life, but it is as though there were a cellophane wall between the soul and the object, and perfect love requires that there should be no wall.

The ultimate goal is to transcend duality—and this is the great point—and that is achieved only at the crown of the head, at the seventh *cakra, sahasrāra,* "the thousand-petaled lotus." Once the *kuṇḍalinī* has arrived at this pinnacle, the dividing membrane is withdrawn from between the soul and its beloved, and both are gone. For there to be an object, there must be a subject of knowledge and a relationship between them. So, with the membrane withdrawn, both the soul and God are extinguished, joined beyond duality, beyond pairs of opposites.

There one finds what we, in our language, can only call identity. And yet it can't be called identity because it is beyond categories altogether. It is this that I want to speak about. With the passage across the line of mystery between the sixth and the seventh *cakras,* something impossible to think of takes place; namely, all phenomenology is transcended, and with that all subjectivity as well. Schopenhauer speaks of this in *The World As Will and Representation.* He says, "If we could only understand how it is that that which is one becomes many, how that which is no thing, becomes things."[29] He calls this paradox the "world knot." If we could understand that, we would understand all, but it cannot be understood.

Yoga of the Body, Mind, and Heart

The yoga that I've been describing is called *rājā yoga,* the great, or kingly, yoga, for a reason. It is remarkably demanding. In fact, it is so strenuous that a sort of preparatory yoga was developed to get you ready to attempt the ascent of the *kuṇḍalinī.* This yoga is called *haṭha;* it is a sort of physical yoga for achieving physical strength, coordination, limberness; you are to stand on your head, twist your back, stretch your legs, and all that—not to achieve illumination but to build a strong body. Sometimes *haṭha* yoga is regarded as prerequisite to *rājā* yoga because *rājā* yoga really demands a great deal of the body, and it is a good idea to build it up first, like a runner conditioning himself for a race.

The irony is that most of the yoga that is taught to people in the West is this sort of yogic calisthenics. You have probably seen the books on how to practice yoga at home—something like doing athletic warm-ups—it's teaching a setting-up exercise. But here we think of *haṭha* as the thing itself rather than a form of preparation.

Of course, not all of us can turn inward and go through this psychological discipline that I have been describing of bringing the *kuṇḍalinī* up the spine through breathing, the specified postures, the meditation, and all. Yet all of us are in action and we can practice a yoga of action as follows: do what you conceive to be your duty without either desire or fear for the fruits, without desire or fear for the fruits either for yourself or for others. This is known as *dharma yoga.*

This is a terrific and terrible teaching. The big difference between its manifestation in the Orient and the way it might be manifest in the West is in this point: in the Orient a person's duty is dictated to him by his society; that is to say, the society imprints on the individual a system of duties that he is expected to render without criticism, whatever they may be.

That is why, in the Bhagavad Gītā, Kṛṣṇa says to Arjuna on the battlefield, "You are a warrior." Arjuna's purpose in life is the *dharma* defined by his class. But in our society we have the idea of self-responsible criticism, self-responsible judgment; every individual is not simply an imprinted robot doing what he is told but a developed conscious, cogitating, criticizing, judging individual self-responsible for his actions—not the good soldier but the good citizen. In relation to what that level of your consciousness tells you is your duty, you are to do it in terms of this doctrine, and you are then practicing the yoga of action.

There are just two more forms of yoga that I want to mention very briefly. One is the yoga of philosophy. Thinking: that is very different from this breathing business that the seated yogi enacts. The yoga of philosophy—or discrimination—*(viveka)* consists in distinguishing between the subject and the object of knowledge: I am not my body, I am the knower of my body; I am not my emotions, I am the knower of my emotions; I am not my thoughts, I am the knower of my thoughts; I am not my ideals and purposes, I am the knower of these. In this way, you drive yourself out the back of the wall, so to say. Through this form of contemplation, you separate yourself from the world of phenomena. The Buddha went one step further: he said that there is no subject of knowledge; you are not that either. Thus you are deprived of every image of yourself, you are beyond all imaging. That is the philosophical form of yoga. In Sanskrit, this is called *jñāna yoga*.

And then there is one other form of yoga: that is the form that we call religion. This is the only yoga in which a god image is involved. This can be any one of these gods I have spoken of, and the yoga consists of loving this god, devoting yourself to the god. This prepares you for going beyond the knowledge of the god. This yoga of religion is called in India *bhakti yoga*, the yoga of devotion and ritual.

Just as the *kuṇḍalinī* has seven levels, so here there are five levels of this love or devotion.

The lowest form of religious love in this system is that of servant to master: "Oh Lord, you are the master, I am your servant. Tell me what to do, and I will do it. What is my duty?" We are all familiar with this mode of religious practice.

The second form of religious love is that of friend to friend, as Kṛṣṇa loved Arjuna and his brothers, the Pāṇḍavas, the heroes of the Mahābhārata; this is love, too, as Christ loved the apostles. This is a higher form of religious readiness—the relationship of inner companion. To be worthy to gain this relationship to the god you must have a more developed religious consciousness than that of the servant. You become a friend of God. God is your companion. You live with him, you think of him all the time, not simply in service once a week or twice a year.

The third level of love is that of parent for child, where the god is the child. This is the image of the Christmas crèche. This image embodies bringing the child-god to life within your own heart. All you know is the cherishing of this little child-god: let's bring it, let's cultivate it, let's help it to grow up.

In the Indian tradition there are a series of charming little stories of Kṛṣṇa as a child—they call him the "butter thief," that naughty little boy, beloved by everybody. His mother one day was told by a friend, "Little Kṛṣṇa has been eating mud." And she goes out and slaps him and opens his mouth to take the mud out and clean his mouth. Then he plays a trick on her. As she is gazing into his mouth, she sees the whole universe there, revealed in a single instant. She didn't know who he had been up to that point, so her hair stood on end. And then he did her another favor: he wiped that recollection out so she should forget it.

There is another, very pretty little anecdote associated with this in *The Gospel of Sri Ramakrishna.*[30] One day, a woman came to this wonderful saint I have been speaking about and said, "Oh master, I don't love God. I know I don't and there is no use in pretending. I don't understand God, I don't understand anything about him. I can't say that I love God."

Ramakrishna said, "Is there no one you love?"

"Yes," she said, "I love my little nephew."

He said, "There you are. In your service to the nephew, you are in the service to your deity."

We find this level of devotion, too, in Kṛṣṇa's advice to the cowherds who were singing praises to Indra, the Lord of Thunder. He says, "What about the cows? Those are your support. Worship them."

Now, all things in the Orient bear the spark of the divine immanent within them, so that in our doings in life we bring forth the divinity. This is a fundamental idea of Oriental yoga—indeed, as I have said, of all Oriental religion. The things we're doing here are the bringing into manifestation of this transcendent realization.

The fourth level of love is that of husband and wife. This is the devotion of the nun, for example, who is the bride of Christ; but it is the level also of husband and wife in their attention and love for each other.

As always, the Indians go one step further again. What is the fifth and highest form of love? It is *illicit* love, where it's nothing but love, and with that you lose your reputation, you lose your job, you may lose your life in madness for love. People who are mad for love that way have lost the world for love and they are the supreme lovers—the way of love culminates in this. That is the kind of love illustrated in the love of Kṛṣṇa and the *gopīs.*

The medieval Bengali poet-composer Jayadeva (c. A.D. 1100), in his masterwork the *Gītā Govinda* (Song of the Cowherd), tells the story that when the boy Kṛṣṇa played his flute in the woods, the milkmaids and young housewives would cock their ears a moment, drop their pots and pans, and then all go running to the wilds. The musician was difficult to find, and the women were always a long time away. Domestic affairs declined; the husbands had no one to prepare their meals; all the routines of the community were falling into disorder.

Now, when they would have searched all day with no visible sign of their beloved trickster, the young women would pause to rest and bathe. Bathing in India is a way of worship. "O goddess, do thou grant," they prayed as they refreshed their tired limbs, "that Kṛṣṇa may be our lord."

One day when they had thus put aside their garments and were splashing in the river, singing little songs in praise of their musician, the boy Kṛṣṇa overheard, and quietly approaching, secretly watched them from a hiding place among the leaves. Then he gathered up their clothing, took it all under his arm, and ascended a tree. The girls finished and came ashore. They were troubled; one discovered Kṛṣṇa in his tree, and all hurried back to the protection of the river Jumna.

Kṛṣṇa laughed. "You must come out," he declared, "and fetch them."

"That is a nice thing for you to ask," they scolded. "Have you no respect for our husbands' honor? We shall tell our parents and your father and mother, and you shall be punished. And then besides," they argued, "it is for your sake we are bathing and keeping vows."

"If that is so," said the boy, "cast away your shame before me and come for your things."

They reasoned among themselves. "He knows all our body and mind," one said. "What shame, after all?" they decided. Yet they came out of the water with downcast eyes.

Kṛṣṇa laughed again. "Now with joined hands," he said, "come forward and get your clothes."

The young women forced Kṛṣṇa to promise that he would dance with them when the rains were finished in the fall. An impatient summer was passed, then one full moon night the flute was heard. The pots were left again, the girls hurried to deck themselves, and the fields were scattered with lively feet making for the edge of the forest. One young woman was captured by her husband, who brought her back to the house and bound her. She set her mind, however, on the lord of the flute and so left her body and came to him first of all. Kṛṣṇa gave her immediate salvation.

The women discovered Kṛṣṇa deep in the forest. "Well," he greeted them, "you have experienced the wonderful night; you have seen the great trees in the moonlight along the beautiful banks of the Jumna. Let that be enough; go home now to your husbands."

Indignant, weeping, scolding, they accused Kṛṣṇa of a cruel deception and threw themselves on his mercy: "Husband, home, and clan we have left and have thought nothing of the reproaches of the world. There is now no one but you to protect us. O Lord, we are enwrapped in love."

Kṛṣṇa by his skill formed a golden terrace in a circle on the Jumna bank, and it was planted all about with plantain trees, hung with garlands of all manner of flowers. The girls retreated to a pool, where they beautified themselves. They brought lutes and cymbals and began to sing and dance, while the Flute Lover stood amongst them twirling them into ecstasy: each imagined him now as entirely her own.

Then he suddenly vanished, taking with him only the beautiful Rādha. The rest were stunned, then frightened. They began to search, and to cry, "Why have you left us, we who have surrendered all?" They inquired of the trees, the beasts, the birds: "Has he passed this way? Have you seen him here—or there?" Then they discovered the prints of his feet and those of a woman going beside. They came to a bed of leaves and discovered near it a jeweled mirror. "Where has he gone?" they asked the mirror; but there was no reply.

Meanwhile Rādha was full of delight and pride. She fancied herself to be the greatest of all. She became so pleased with herself that she asked her lover to take her up onto his shoulders. The minute she set her foot to mount, he vanished, and she stood alone with outstretched hands.

Here the young women found her. They were as glad as though they had recovered the first half of their treasure. They embraced the girl—all embraced her and laughed and wept. Then she joined them in the hopeless quest. At last, faint and disheveled, weeping and aching with love, they all sat down on the Jumna bank to cry.

Kṛṣṇa reappeared. "Like monks quitting their homes for God," he said, "you have come to me. You have suffered all the trials. How can I reward you?" Then he began to play.

The young women, the *gopīs,* arose and danced. Kṛṣṇa made his appearance manifold and danced with each of them in the ring. So they whirled—the blue-black Kṛṣṇa and the fair-skinned *gopīs*—like a necklace of sapphire and gold. Some played their lutes and sang. Mind and body were both forgotten. When one of the *gopīs* stopped Kṛṣṇa's flute with her hand and continued the flute song with her own voice, the god-hero was ravished, like a child discovering its own face in a glass.

Deities descended from heaven to watch the wonderful dance; the water and wind stood still. But when four watches yet remained of the night, Kṛṣṇa ceased and declared the time had come for all to return to their homes. "Meditate always upon me as yogis do," he said, "that I may be ever near you."[31]

The sanctioned love of husband and wife involves life duties of all kinds, but this divine passion is sheer, unbounded love. The rapture of the *gopīs* resembles the *amour* of the twelfth-century Provençal troubadours. Troubadour love was illicit love, dangerous love; it was love, not in terms of the social order but in terms of an irresistible attraction of the heart that has gone out of control, and that's the madness of the hermit, the madness of the person crazy with love for God.

Likewise, in the broad domain of Islam, this was the era when the passionate love play of Joseph and Potiphar's wife (Yusuf and Zuleika) was celebrated by Nizāmī (A.D. 1140–1203) and the other Muslim poets of "the double truth":

> Who made the Law their outer garment
> And the mystic Path their inner garment.

In Japan, too, at this time the courtly game of romantic love was being played in a mystical ambient supplied by the Buddhist concept of the oneness of existences. It was the period of the "cloud gallants" and "flower maidens," and the "tenderness, pity, and sympathy" *(aware)* of their hearts, penetrated by the pathos of nature, who are celebrated by Lady Murasaki in *The Tale of Genji. Mono no aware o shiru*—"to know *(shiru)* the pathos *(aware)* of things *(mono)*," to have a heart open to that sense of compassion that is the essence of Buddhahood: this was the Far Eastern counterpart of the Gentle Heart of Provence and the divine rapture of the *gopīs.*

For in all of these traditions, marriage was symbolic of "the Law"—and love's compulsion, of "the mystic Path." Thus, for one brief shining moment, in every castle of the world from the English Channel to the Persian Gulf and to the Sea of Japan, the one song was variously ringing of the liege man of Love, locally accommodated to the Christian, Muslim, Hindu, and Buddhist modes of instrumentation.

The Round of Sorrow[32]

Birth and Rebirth

All of the traditions that came out of India—Jainism, Hinduism, and Buddhism—center on the idea of reincarnation. This is just as fundamental to Indian mythological thinking as our idea of Judgment, Heaven, and Hell is to our tradition. The notion is that the soul—what I will call the reincarnating monad—puts on bodies and takes them off, over and over again, as a person puts on and removes clothing.

What is the function of the body? The function of the body is to put your *jīva,* your deathless soul, into the realm of temporal experience. The body is meant to stimulate the soul with challenges, and then, once the *jīva* has assimilated the possibilities inherent in the experiences of this lifetime, the body is flung away and another body is taken on. According to this view, you are born into a particular caste or social position that is appropriate to the readiness of your soul. The notion is that, in a manner of speaking, you chose your parents. The soul is ready for a certain type of experience, so it will be born into a family that will provide those experiences.

Now, the individual soul may resist these experiences, in which case it fails to benefit from this lifetime. In this case, the soul is thrown right back like an undersized fish until the soul has learned the lesson. The ultimate goal for the soul is to reach the point where it does not need to put on a body anymore. It is released, to be not anybody, anything—to become one with the light.

What is it that brings the soul back, putting on bodies like a shopper at Macy's trying on scarves? It is desire and fear. You have a desire for life; you have a fear of death. When you absolutely quench desire and fear, those things by which all of us live, then there is no life. That is the ultimate aim of all the yogas. Of course you can go through all kinds of exercises and think you have gotten rid of desire and fear, but the very fact that you are trying to get rid of them is a desire. This is the funny twist that every monk runs up against: the harder you try not to want, the more you're *wanting* not to want, and so you are in a double bind. The illumination comes when you are least ready. I think we have this in our Christian imagery, too—very often Christ comes when you are not looking for him, and you must be ready. A sage once wrote, "Beware of the passing of Jesus, for he does not come again." This moment of real illumination comes when you're not quite watching for it; often, when you are striving you are actually blocking it.

Jīva, the Sanskrit word for this reincarnating entity, is related to the Latin *viva.* This is the living force that keeps putting bodies on. Now, on a higher level, since all beings are manifestations of that ultimate being, *Brahman-ātman,* all *jīvas* are manifestations of the *ātman,* and if you will realize that this is *nirvāṇa,* you will lose that will to get loose and you will be loose while alive. That business of being in balance while moving in the world is the key to this. Now, this is a balance; one reason that athletics and things like music performance and dance performance are so helpful as disciplines is that to do these things well you have to be both doing them and not doing them; there has to be a kind of relaxation and turning the activity over to the body, to the performing power, so that your consciousness rides along with it. That is very much like the saintly attitude. The still point rests in the middle and the activity swirls round about, and you are both the nirvanic point and the activity. The point where the Buddha sat is called the immovable point, but it is the world just as the hub is part of the wheel, and that's because of the non-dual realization we get on the other side.

These realizations are wonderfully paradoxical. Depending on the person's balance and stress in his life and yearnings, he will find himself in accord with this, that, or another system, and that's what all these systems are for. In Buddhism these are called Buddha realms. Each has a different kind of discipline to try to get you to feel, I'm there already, this is it, it's all one. This is the final realization, *nirvāṇa.*

Nirvāṇa literally means "blown out"; the image is that once one has realized one's unity with what is called the Buddha mind—this is the Buddhist conception of *Brahman*—then one's individual ego is extinguished like a candle flame, and one becomes one with the great solar light.

But when you get over there, you realize, I was here all the time. That's all, folks; we're there, and there is no place to go, and this is, basically, it. As Dr. Daisetz Suzuki, the Japanese Zen master, once said, "This world—with all its faults, all its crime, all its horror, all its banality, all its stupidity—is the golden lotus world." But you have to learn to see it in that dimension.

There is an Indian fable of three beings who drank from a river: one was a god, and he drank ambrosia; one was a man, and he drank water; and one was a demon, and he drank filth. What you get is a function of your own consciousness. So, finally, the lower cakras and the higher cakras are the same. This gives a kind of violence and power to Indian mysticism and spirituality that is a bit horrifying.

The Horror

These days, many Westerners have read the Bhagavad Gītā, the *Song of the Lord,* which is the nuclear work of Indian spiritual life. The Gītā is a passage of some eighteen chapters in the midst of the great Indian epic the Mahābhārata, a work eight times as long as the *Odyssey* and *Iliad* combined. In this sprawling tale of war and love is this little jewel of spiritual revelation.

To sum it up very briefly it is as follows: The young warrior-prince Arjuna is the leader of an army, along with his brothers, the Pāṇḍavas. They have lost their possessions—their kingdom and even their shared bride—in a dice game with their cousins, the Kauravas, who are the leaders of the opposing army. Now, Arjuna's charioteer is his friend Kṛṣṇa, who is an incarnation of the god Viṣṇu; Kṛṣṇa is the lord of the title of the book, in that he is both a king and an avatar of the lord of the world. Though he is God incarnate himself, he is playing the role of charioteer at this cataclysmic battle between the armies led by these two bands of brothers. In the moments of quiet before the fighting, with both armies waiting for his trumpet call to start, Arjuna says to Kṛṣṇa, "Drive me out between the two armies before I let the battle start; I just want to see for a minute."

So Kṛṣṇa does drive Arjuna out. Arjuna sees on both sides men whom he admires, men whom he loves, and he drops his bow. He goes pale and says, "Better that I should die here than that I should let loose this battle fury."

His friend, the god, looks at him and says, "Whence comes this cowardice? You have lost your mind; you have lost your equilibrium. You are a warrior, and the highest goal of a warrior is a just war." Now, all wars are just from both sides, always. Kṛṣṇa, having the divine long view, understands this. "So get in there and fight. Did you think *you* were going to kill these people? They are already dead!" Then he touches Arjuna's eye and Arjuna sees his friend Kṛṣṇa transformed into the lord of the world. He is a tremendous, monstrous divinity, with many mouths with great tusks in these mouths. In this expanded vision, Arjuna sees both armies flying into these mouths and smashing like grapes, and the blood pouring down from the maws like spilled wine.

Arjuna's hair lifts and he says, "Who are you?"

His former companion answers and says, "I am Kāla. I am black time, who am here for the end of the world. I am licking up mankind. Now," he says, his appearance returning to its normal blue-skinned calm, "did you think you were going to kill these men? They are already dead, as I told you. Those forms that you kill are mortal, but the immortal portion is untouched. What was never born never dies. Rains do not wet it; fire does not burn it. So get in there and seem to be doing things. You are to be the instrument of destiny itself."

It is this section of the Gīta that J. Robert Oppenheimer seems to have had in mind when he uttered his famous words on viewing the first test of the atomic bomb: "I am become Death, the destroyer of worlds."

The World Soul[33]

Māyā

When we look at the contemporary Western conception of the individual, of the self, it is predicated around the psychology of Sigmund Freud, Jacob Adler, and Carl Jung.

Now, there are at least three points that make it possible to speak of Eastern religious practice—yoga—and our own depth psychology in the same breath. The first is the recognition that all of the pantheons of the world, the divinities, the heavens and hells, and so forth, are seen in yoga as projections of psychological images. That is to say, what we think of normally as metaphysics and theology are interpreted as psychology, as a function of the mind.

The second point is that the energies that are expressed and rendered in these images are the energies that determine the direction and the course of a life. The images that fascinate—fascinate because they link into one's own dynamic processes—are seen, in a sense, as images of destiny. They are images that determine your existence. This is what in India is termed *māyā,* that image world of illusions that so often move us against our best interests and even our intentions. *Māyā* is the world of that rippling pond we spoke of, the fractured, sparkling image of reality that is no reality but only its broken surface.

And the third and last point is that, with the coming to consciousness of the implications of these images, the penetrations of the energies to the energy sources, one can illuminate one's life, relax it, and give it a sense of spontaneity and scope in its movements that can be termed "release," release from the compulsive force of destiny, and the rendition of a state of free determination. This is the idea behind the great heaven-ascending ladder of the seven *cakras,* the centers of the *kuṇḍalinī* yoga. It is also the basic idea behind psychoanalysis—that once one has brushed aside the webs of subconscious compulsion, one is released to the freedom of being a subject.

It is when the inner light—the ultimate light that is no light, that is

Brahman-ātman—comes into manifestation that this *māyā* veil is passed. I once saw a little kitten that found itself reflected in a mirror. The mirror was without a frame and was standing against a wall. This little creature saw itself in the mirror and thought it was another. Its back went up in the usual way, and its hair stood out, and it began stalking its opponent. And as it showed aggression, so did the other. It went at it and at it—and then, suddenly, it got past the mirror and there was no other animal there. Then it came back and there was its enemy again, so it went back to the attack. This went on and on; it was a marvelous thing to see. Then the kitten went the other direction around the mirror, and once again the enemy disappeared. Then it started looking behind the mirror for what should have been there, and of course there was nothing there but itself. It had lost its object; it didn't even think of itself really as a subject. And I thought, Well, good gosh, this is an image of *māyā* exactly.

No one can say what *māyā* is because on this side of *māyā* we live within its atmosphere, as fish do in water. But on the far side of *māyā,* there is no one there to know, to observe our state objectively. So when you come back—from reincarnation, say, or from a transcendent experience—it is just as mysterious as anything you can imagine.

Māyā is said to have three powers. The first power is called the obscuring power: it shuts out, as it were, the white light of eternity. *Māyā* operates like a mask or curtain over truth.

Or you might think of *māyā* as a prism: the white light strikes the prism and is broken into myriad rays. This is second, or projecting, power. Here the forms of the world are projected, just as the light through the prism. Now, no one who had never seen white light could imagine white light from looking at the seven multicolored lights.

However, if these seven are arranged on a disk, and the disk is made to spin, you will see the white light again. So we say that *māyā* has a third power, the revealing power. *Māyā,* in mythological language, is the mother of the world, creation in the feminine aspect. The white light is neither masculine nor feminine, because it transcends all dualities. On this side of the prism, however—this side of *māyā*—we find male and female, and all of the other pairs of opposites. This is the base of the matriarchal religions. All forms, even the form of God the Father, are within the womb of Māyā the Mother. We are within her womb. It is the womb of space, time, and causal relationships, what Kant calls the "a priori forms of sensibility." This is exactly *māyā,* and this is exactly why Schopenhauer, following Kant, was able to interpret the Indian terminology in Kantian terms, point for point. *Brahman* equals the Kantian *Ding an sich,* that which is no thing, which is only itself. It transcends all categories. Both the forms of sensibility and the categories of thought are enclosed within the womb of Māyā, including God, as we speak of him and think of him and name him as well.

In *kuṇḍalinī* yoga, the lord of the world is perceived at the sixth *cakra,* below which all belongs to Māyā's domain. There is a lovely little fifteenth-century Madonna in the Musée de Cluny in Paris. She sits with the Christ child on her arm, and the globe of the universe in her left hand. Her chest can be opened out like a cabinet, and within one sees God the Father, God the Son, God the Holy Ghost, and the whole choir of heaven. The whole imagery of the heavens and hells is enclosed within her, and this image is exactly the image of Māyā, the mother. Hers, then, is the power of projection, the creative power, as it were, of illusion.

Within her domain, we come to the imagery of the lord of the world. And this imagery may be in either masculine or feminine form. It is one of the curiosities of our Western religion that we insist on the ultimate divine being visualized in masculine form. Since the ultimate is beyond pairs of opposites, why this? The Indians speak of one's "chosen" deity; one's own peculiar psychology is what determines the image that will speak to one most eloquently and carry one onto the higher planes.

Destroyers and Creators

Now, in traditional mythologies around the world—the biblical traditions notwithstanding—the prime divine representation of the soul of the world is the Goddess herself. And with respect to living beings, she is both their mother and their consumer—she brings us forth, she takes us back. And from the standpoint of the individual afraid of death, she is therefore a horrendous aspect. But insofar as our worship of her can relieve us of the commitment to our bodies, and relieve us of the fear of death—give us rather the sense of returning to our source—she can be said to free us from this little ego ring that binds us in.

In India, in one of her main aspects, Kālī (Kṛṣṇa's Kāla in her more typical female form), she is depicted as absolutely black: *kālī* means "black." She is that which is beyond all imaging, that darkness, that mystery out of which all things come, and back into which they go.

She is depicted as standing on the prostrate white form of her spouse, Śiva. He is represented in this dead form as inert, in the sense of being symbolic of that transcendent force that begets us through the goddess. This is the couple that is represented in the most common object of worship throughout India, namely the symbol of the *liṅgam-yoni,* the male and female organs in conjunction. And this symbol is always represented as though the *liṅgam* was penetrating the *yoni* from beneath, as though the abyssal mystery were injecting the energy of life into this womb of the world within which we are. And standing before such an image, we are to think of ourselves as contemplating the mystery of the pouring of energy, the energy of being, into the sphere of being that is the womb of the goddess.

Figure 7. Kālī, c. 1832

Now, in these religions of the East, we do not have the idea of a personal creator who determines to create and so brings about an initial moment in cosmic history, and finally is there when the world ends. There is no beginning for time; there is no end for time. Time-thinking is thinking involved in this womb-world; such thought does not touch the problem of eternity.

In this view, eternity is not a long time; rather, it is another dimension. It is that dimension to which time-thinking shuts us. And so there never was a creation. Rather, there is a continuous creating going on. This energy is pouring into every cell of our being right now, every board and brick of the buildings we sit in, every grain of sand and wisp of wind. It is *aum,* the sound of the universe, that sound that is not made by two things rubbing together.

This is a sense of the whole universe as alive, the whole universe as a moment, you might say, of procreation, and that is the sense of this wonderful mystery of the image. But it can be represented also in the form of a god and goddess in embrace. This is the Śiva-Śakti image, the god and his *śakti,* or his consort. This wonderful word *śakti* has two simultaneous meanings: first, it applies to the female in relation to the male; a man's wife, his consort, is his *śakti.*

Second, and more fundamentally, the word means "energy." The male, you might say, is a placid being, and what he wants deep inside is just to be left alone. And then this aromatic mystery goes past, and he is stirred. As James Joyce says in *Finnegans Wake,* "She whispers to him of such and such and so and so." And he thinks, Well, it would be nice to go at it again. And so we have a new world, another world. He is stirred and becomes active.

This is quite contrary to our normal Western view, and also to the Chinese view, where the female is recognized as the mask principle, the inert object, and the male is the active subject. Here the male is the inert one and the woman is the activator. Ramakrishna speaks of the male and female principles as water quiet and water rippled. We have this same image in the first verse of the Bible:

> In the beginning God created the heaven and the earth.
> And the earth was without form, and void; and darkness was upon

> the face of the deep. And the Spirit of God moved upon the face of the waters.
>
> And God said, Let there be light: and there was light.[34]

It is that activation of the water that demarks the world creation. And in that act of water, what we see are lights coming and going, coming and going—the ripples on the pond. Those lights are ourselves, and we think of ourselves as this light to be preserved: here I am; oh dear, now I'm gone.

The Eastern texts tell us, rather, "Don't identify yourself with that little shimmering light. Identify yourself with that source of light that is reflected in this shimmer with which you have identified yourself."

As we have seen, the goddess may be pictured as a mother—as a Madonna. Then again, she may be pictured—and again, we have seen that she often is—as a quite horrendous, horrifying phenomenon. This is Kālī, black time the devourer. She stands in a heroic attitude with her tongue out long, sometimes down to her waist, red and threatening, to lick back the blood of her creatures. It is she who gives birth; it is she who swallows back the world. One right hand will say, "Don't be afraid, nothing's happening." The other will either be in the boon-bestowing posture or hold a little bowl of milk-rice. She is the Annapūrṇā, the cornucopia—the one full of food, giving, giving, giving of her abundance. Then we look to her left hands: one will have a sword of death, and another will be holding a head that she has just cut off. And in fact, it is to her that most of the great sacrifices took place: beheadings of animals and human beings. The idea was to place the severed head immediately on her altar so that the fresh foaming blood, as ambrosia, would flow back to her. And at her shrine you will see the channel to carry the blood back to its source in her. She will always have a necklace of skulls. And her kilt will be of arms and legs that have been amputated, and we are to address her as "our dear mother."

In the West, we tend to make our beneficent divinities beneficent, and our malignant ones malignant. The main point in these Eastern images is that both terms are present in the same image, as they are in life. In his wonderful *Tristan,* Gottfried von Strassburg says, "They tell me there are those who seek only happiness and peace. Let God give them peace. I seek the life that has both bitterness and sweetness simultaneously."[35]

And that's what we get in these wonderful Indian images. And the power with which this dual aspect of life is rendered, and we are asked to acquiesce in it, is something that is very telling when one experiences it. The consort of this goddess is Śiva, probably the oldest worshiped divinity now extant. He is the lord of the *liṅgam;* that is to say, he is the symbol of the procreating God. And he is shown in some later images in two forms simultaneously. The Goddess who is our mother is seated upon him. And he is in two forms beneath her—one form turned away and another turned toward her. The form turned toward her has his eyes open, and that is properly Śiva. The form turned away has the eyes closed; that form is our friend Śava the corpse. The one turned away has absorbed both Śiva and Śakti back into himself.

These represent the two attitudes of yoga. One may have the yoga of world quitting, leaving the world. This is, as they say in the Upaniṣads, the way of the fire, which carries us to the Sun door, and then out into eternity. In contrast to that is the yoga of world affirmation: the ever-returning father principle, fructifying the world, returning, returning, returning. This is the way of smoke, which leads us to the Moon, which dies and is resurrected, over and over again.

Remember, there are two images of eternal life. One is the image of the eternal return, and the other is the passage out of this circle of time altogether. The way of smoke or the way of the flame. Śiva, in the attitude of the *liṅgam,* represents the returning principle, the world-creating, world-preserving, world-generating principle.

In his other attitude as yogi—and Śiva is the Lord of Yoga, as we remember from meeting him in that Mohenjo Daro seal—he is covered with ashes, with unkempt hair hanging down in matted locks. He hasn't taken a bath in ten thousand years. He has garlands of serpents that drink from a skull. He has his trident in hand, but he is concentrated deeply in yoga, quitting the world. He represents the attitude of the destroyer of *māyā*-as-illusion. You see fellows like this in India, carrying Śiva's trident, covered in dirt and ash, with long, long, matted hair. Fantastic.

Another form of a much more genial sort is Viṣṇu.

Viṣṇu is the more erotic, world-affirming deity. He enters the world in love as an incarnation whenever the world is in trouble. There are many such incarnations—Rāma and Kṛṣṇa are the best known to us. From the Hindu standpoint, Christ would be an incarnation of Viṣṇu. When a

Christian missionary goes into an Indian village and speaks of incarnation, of God coming in human form into this world out of love, the locals say, "What's the news?"

The erotic lore of the five stages of love—this lore is associated with Viṣṇu.

He is generally represented in human form reclining on a serpent. This serpent's name is Ananta, which means "unending." Its seven cobra heads arch over Viṣṇu like an umbrella, and it is floating on the cosmic ocean, that symbol of the world energy out of which all proceeds. This is the ocean we read about in the first verse of the Bible. The water, the serpent, and the god are equivalent figures in elemental, animal, and human form respectively. They all symbolize that dark source out of which all comes. One may think of that source as the bottom of our pond. And then one may think of a lotus coming up through the waters of that pond and opening on the surface. So it is in the Viṣṇu image. Viṣṇu is dreaming. He is dreaming the dream of the world. He is dreaming his own *māyā* world, and it emerges from his navel in the form of a lotus. When the dream ends, it recedes again, only to reemerge with the beginning of the next dream. This is the image with which Kṛṣṇa humbled Indra.

Figure 8. Viṣṇu, Brahmā, and Lakṣmi

Now, this lotus is the symbol of the universe itself as divinely given.

The word *lotus—padmā*—is the name too of the goddess who is Viṣṇu's consort, his *śakti*. (She is also known as Lakṣmī.) Undoubtedly, Padmā the goddess was originally that lotus herself. She is the world. Her womb is the lotus of the world within. Interestingly, with the patriarchal emphasis of the latter Indian tradition, she was removed from the lotus, and you see her now in the images as the good Indian wife massaging her sleeping husband's foot. But there is a little secret there: it is that massage which is stimulating the dream. She is still Śakti. And what is he dreaming about? Her.

But in her place on the lotus there is now put this masculine god who's actually a rather late invention: Brahmā. There he sits, with his four faces observing the four directions, imagining that he is creating the world.

Brahmā is a personification of the consciousness of *Brahman*. Brahmā is a god, a personification—a symbol as we are all, in this manner of thinking, symbols—of that eternal principle. All gods and creatures are secondary manifestations. Brahmā manifests *Brahman* in its creator aspect, projecting the world that is *māyā*. Viṣṇu and Śiva are simply other manifestations. And each one of these personifications represents a different inflection of the truth, the pure light that is *Brahman*.

These, then, are the three deities that we find most in representations of later Indian religion. You have Brahmā, who is the creator in the light world, the world above the surface of *māyā*—he is all light and radiance. There is Viṣṇu, the dreamer of the cosmic dream. Of course, just as all the figures in your dream are aspects and portions of yourself, so are we—as figures in Viṣṇu's dream—aspects or portions of Viṣṇu. We are all identical with Viṣṇu. And the goal of our yoga is going to be to realize ourselves in that identity. And then there is Śiva in his form as the *liṅgam* in relation to the goddess Śakti, or as the yogi. (Later, we will discover Śiva in yet another aspect: Śiva Naṭarāja, the dancer of the cosmic dance.)

When these three deities, Brahmā, Viṣṇu, and Śiva, are put together, you have a *trimūrti*, the three-formed god, or trinity: Brahmā is the creator, Viṣṇu the preserver, and Śiva the destroyer. But actually Śiva is also creator—he reunites us with the original source of creation. And Brahmā and Viṣṇu are also destroyers, trapping us in the world of *māyā*, illusion.

This sort of secondary assignment often happens in mythology. When deities of two different orders and different origins come together in a unified system, they have to be assigned duties, like employees from two newly merged banks. So you have a secondary departmentalization of the gods.

You get this throughout the classical tradition. Poseidon and Zeus, for example, both started out as master deities—Zeus among the Achaean Greeks and Poseidon among the Cretans and the Aegean peoples—and when the two traditions are brought together, they are given assignments.

Just how old are these images? Also, are they native to India? This is a very deep and very interesting question and problem. As we said, the earliest dates that we have for the culture world in India connect with the Dravidian culture in the Indus Valley, from the period of around 2500 to 1500 B.C. This is the period, just to the west, of ancient Akkad, Sumer, and the Mesopotamian city-states—the period of Sargon I and Hammurabi. In Egypt it is the end of the Late and beginning of the Middle Kingdom.

Most interestingly, it is the period of the great palace period in Crete. It is worthwhile to note that Śiva's symbols are the trident, the bull, and the *liṅgam.* These are exactly the symbols of Poseidon, who was, understandably, the principal divinity of ancient sea-bound Crete. It seems clear, beyond a reasonable doubt, that both of these worlds, Crete and India, received their civilization from the much older high civilized domain of the Near East. The archaeological record in Iran, Syria, and Turkey goes back thousands of years earlier than 2500 B.C. We have evidence of a recognizable civilization at Çatal Hüyük in Anatolia going back as far as 8000 B.C.—at least five millennia prior to Mohenjo Daro and Harappa. This is almost as many years as mark the time from India's first civilization to the present. And these divinities that are worshiped today in India, and whose implications have been developed in these glorious philosophies, have their roots back there. India has continued and developed an inspiration with respect to a poetic image, to the order of the world, that traces its roots back to the first of the great high cultures.

What do we have in this image in the way of a worldview? We have an image of a totally impersonal power—*Brahman*—that moves the world through great cycles, as that lotus comes from Viṣṇu and goes back again, comes and goes in a great cycle like a flower's blooming. So the universe comes and goes.

The principal image is of the Four Ages of the World, as we know them from Hesiod: The Age of Gold, of Silver, of Bronze, and of Iron. In India it is the image of the Age of the Four, the Three, the Two, and the One. In the Age of the Four, the Goddess of Virtue—the original sacred cow—was standing on all four legs. This was the Golden Age. At that time human beings were born in couples. You didn't have to look for your soul's companion. Furthermore, the rivers ran with wine and milk, and the trees rippled in beautiful melodies. And the whole world, the soil itself, was sweet, was sugar to eat. People were very happy in those days, and they didn't have to think, What should I do? They acted virtuously automatically.

Then there came the Age of Silver, or the Three, when the Cow of Virtue was standing on only three legs. This time people were not quite so virtuous; they had to pause a minute to think, How should it be done? What should I do? But they would act virtuously even so. They were not as tall or beautiful, but from our point of view now they would be divine.

Then comes the Age of the Two, when the Cow of Virtue is standing on only two legs. Well, you know a cow can't stand terribly well on two legs. So at this time a prop is brought into being, and this is the period of the scriptures, of little writings that tell you how to behave. This is the period of the coming of religion into the world. Religion was unnecessary before because people acted spontaneously, righteously, and correctly; now they stand corrected.

Finally, of course, there comes the Age of the One, when the cow is on only a single leg. This is our unfortunate time, the age of the mixture of castes, when nobody knows his own true nature. And the worst of it is that people won't read the scriptures, and when they do they don't understand them. This is an age of deterioration, and very rapid deterioration. And if—from the traditional perspective—you want to have any proof of the deterioration, just look at everything that we call progress: it is an exteriorization of life; the machines are taking over. And everything that we in the West consider to be evidence of progress is, in terms of this ancient tradition, evidence of decline. So the world is getting worse.

Once the world has gotten to be just a kind of porridge of indistinguishable nonentities, with no one knowing or following their *dharma,* then Viṣṇu will take the dream back, the lotus will recede, and it will all be gone. Then, after a period of incubation, it will come forth again in its glory. So there is nothing you can do about it, friends. That's the way things are.

There is no such thing as initiative. You cannot do anything that has not been done a million times before, because there is this eternal recurrence. There is no point for the individual to make a specific effort. His real function is to obey the laws of the universe as communicated to him by his society. And if he can't do that, he becomes a nothing and just disintegrates.

In classical Indian sociology, the castes are compared to the limbs of a body. The *brahmin* caste is the head; the *kṣatriya,* or governing, caste is the shoulders and arms; the *vaiśya,* the merchant caste, is the torso; and the laboring caste, the *śūdra,* is the legs. What would happen to a body if the feet said, "I want to be the head"? or the head said, "I want to be the heart"? What do we call that when it happens in a body? We call it cancer. Likewise, what we call democracy is, from this standpoint, cancer.

There is, however, a very special occasion when the caste differentiations can be transcended; certain kinds of worship when one goes past caste. In these circumstances, one has gone past the realm of *māyā* altogether and united oneself with the transcendent power of *Brahman.*

When Kṛṣṇa appears to Arjuna as the world devourer, the point is—among other points—that we are all that Kāla, with all that life and death immanent inside us. Kṛṣṇa gives instruction of how to act when in possession of this knowledge, and here's the formula: act without fear or desire for the fruits of the action. Act without fear or desire either for yourself or for others but simply proceed in the order of life. In the ultimate illumination, all pairs of opposites are transcended, are left behind. Act in the knowledge that this world as we know and experience it is the perfect lotus world—*this* is *nirvāṇa.* The actions we take, whatever they are, are the actions of the divine power.

This can be carried one step further, as is always true in Indian mystic thought: the actions of lust, the actions of pleasure are also yoga. Thus you have this formula: yoga is yoga, delight is yoga. The whole world as it lives is a manifestation of this radiant mystery, and we do not see it.

The Individual in Oriental Myth[36]

The Mask and the Actor

The subject of the traditional Oriental concept of the individual is somewhat difficult because, at least as I see the problem, the idea of the individual as we understand it in the European Western world does not exist in the Orient.

Carl Jung speaks in his works of the integration of the personality and uses the word *individuation* rather frequently. And to make clear what he means, he points out that each one of us is invited by his society to play a certain role, a certain social function. These roles he calls *personae,* from the Latin word for the masks worn by Roman actors.[37] We all have to put on a mask of some sort in order to function in the society. And even those who choose *not* to function in the society, to revolt from the society, put on masks too. They wear certain insignia that indicate, "I am in revolt."

One can be impressed by a persona, by a mask. For example, if one meets a person and is talking to him and thinks one is beginning to establish some kind of rapport and then learns—let us say—that this is the distinguished ambassador from such and such a country, the mask comes in front of that person, and a certain awe creeps into your relationship to him. This person takes on in your mind what Jung calls a *mana* personality, a personality with magical powers. So you are not talking directly to him, you relate through this persona.

In order to be individuated, in order to be an individual, we must learn to distinguish between the self and the masks that we wear. Moreover, each mask goes very deep; it includes moral ideas. It includes judgment systems. Essentially, the persona is a set of archetypes for action that have been impressed upon us by our society.

I take Jung's idea of individuation as a rather clean-cut example of an Occidental ideal that one should put on the mask and take it off. When you come home in the evening, are you still Mr. President or do you leave that in the office? If you keep your mask on, we would call you a stuffed shirt. In such a person, the personality gradually disappears into the ideal image of the role. This is a particular disaster if one becomes impressed by one's own mask. Here we have a real mirage phenomenon: there is nobody there.

The typical ideal in the Orient is that one *should* become identified with the mask. The whole approach to education throughout India and East Asia is to believe what you are told, do what you are told, not to ask questions. For an Occidental teaching Oriental students, this attitude is absolutely bewildering in its submissiveness. For an Oriental teaching

Occidental students, likewise, the challenges are sharp. There is no respect for the professor *qua* professor here. Western students expect to be able to ask questions, to question the professor's assumptions.

This isn't just a cultural difference; it is a difference of metaphysical assumptions as well.

As Dante wandered through the hell pits in the *Inferno,* he recognized all of his friends there—as we should recognize ours if we happened to go to Hell. Proceeding through Purgatory and even Heaven, he knew who those people were. Their individual personalities were preserved even in the afterworld. In the *Odyssey* and the *Aeneid,* the heroes have the same experience. To us, the personality is a permanent, immutable entity. It *is* you. You are born once, you live once: you are that. We identify the spirit with the body.

In the hells and heavens of the Buddhists, or Hindus, or Jains, you could not recognize anybody. They are not the same person they were on Earth. Also, neither heaven nor hell is considered to be a terminal destination. They are both merely stops in the round of reincarnation, *saṁsāra.* The heavens are rewards for a successful incarnation, and the hells are like penal institutions, rehabilitating the soul so that it doesn't make the same mistakes in the next round. In Western terms, they are purgatories.

Let me make a point here. The hero in Europe—in the Greek tragedies, in Dante's *Commedia Divina,* in Jung's idea of the self, or in Joyce's novels—is *this* individual, *this* temporal being, here and now. In India and East Asia, the hero is the reincarnating monad, that entity that goes through bodies, putting them on and taking them off as clothes from one incarnation to the next. This is a continuing theme in the Orient: You are not this body. You are not this ego. You are to think of this as merely something put on to be thrown away again. A fundamental distinction here between our European concept of the individual and that of let us say India and the Far East is that the reincarnating principle makes quite unimportant this particular temporal phenomenon that is now you. The ego concept is both expanded and annihilated, so that one's self is not identified with this temporal phenomenon here and now but with the reincarnating principle.

Of course, what each faith believes the monad to be differs. What is it that we incarnate?

One of the most impressive and wondrous things about the Oriental religions is the concept of the round of existence, these eons that come and go so that worlds come into being and worlds go out of being. This is an idea that originated very long ago in the Near East. As you know our civilizations—whether Occidental or Oriental—have all derived from a Near Eastern base. It was in the great zone of Palestine, Syria, Persia, and Iraq that the earliest agricultural and pastoral communities developed. From these there spread forth this pastoral agrarian society on which the later civilizations are based. Then, as I have mentioned, about 3500 B.C., the priests recognized mathematically calculable movements of the five visible planets, the Sun, and the Moon. And they developed the idea of a mathematical order underlying the whole universe, an order of ever-turning cycles. We have eons mathematically calculated so that after a certain long passage of time, the whole world dissolves and it comes into being again and then it dissolves.

The Greek Hesiod gives us a version of this idea in the four great ages of Gold, Silver, Bronze, and Iron; they come forth and then they go again. In the *Eddas* of the medieval Germanic peoples, the world comes into being and goes out of being.

In the Orient, we have the image of the sacred cow, the Goddess of Virtue, through the Four Ages, standing first on four legs, then three, then two, and now, in the dissolute age we live in, attempting to stand on one.

Throughout India and the Far East this is so. Now when the world does that, when you have this pattern of eternal recurrence, there is nothing you or I can do to change the situation; we're just along for the ride. Individual initiative is of no use whatsoever. It has no value whatsoever. It is an intrusion upon the scene. Just as the Sun rises on schedule and sets on schedule, as the Moon waxes and wanes, and as the plants grow and die, so must you live.

In India this idea is called *dharma,* the idea of that duty, that virtue which is yours as the result of your birth. This *dharma* is understood in terms of caste; that is to say, each order of society has its very strict rules, and you live according to the rules of this order you were born to. It is thought that as a result of earlier birth, you are perfectly ready to be born on that level—a *brahmin,* a *kṣatriya,* a *vaiśya,* a *śūdra,* an ant, a god. Consequently, the moral system—the persona that is supplied you by your social group—is perfectly appropriate to your character, otherwise you would not have been born on that level.

Thus there is no need for a god to judge you and put you in your spot. This happens automatically, as if by specific gravity. The spiritual weight of your soul determines what level of the social order you will come in on, and your duty is simply to do as told, to embody perfectly the ideal of that order. There are old texts—the Laws of Manu and the Institutes of Viṣṇu—that give a detailed enumeration of how you are to behave, how long your sleeves are to be, how many times you are to sneeze in the morning. Every little detail of life is described and prescribed to an iota, and the opportunity to think, What would I like to do now? What would I like to be?—those sorts of questions were not allowed. The slightest infraction was rigorously punished. The society was very serious about this. A *śūdra* who had, by accident perhaps, heard the words of the Vedas, which only the members of the *brahmin* caste are advanced enough to hear, was condemned to have boiling lead poured into each of his ears. One can imagine that such a punishment would be likely to send the monad off on another spin of the wheel of incarnation.

In the farther East, in China and Japan, there is the idea of the Tao, the way. This cosmic order is described in terms different from those of India, but nevertheless amounts to essentially the same thing: namely, that there is a cosmic rhythm, a cosmic order, and that order is intrinsic to our nature, so the real goal of life is to know how to function in unison with the Tao so that our spontaneity is the spontaneity of nature itself. It is a noble, wonderful ideal. It is an ideal of self-giving. The idea of ego in these societies is regarded as the diabolical principle, the negative principle. In fact ego is given no opportunity whatsoever to develop.

In the Indian philosophies there is a very well known classification of the goals for which men live. These are called the four ends of life. There are three goals for which people live in the world, in society; and there is one for which people leave society and go into the forest. The three aims for which people live in society are (1) *dharma,* which is virtue or duty, the idea that you should perform the laws imposed upon you by your caste; (2) *artha,* which is achievement or aggression; and (3) *kāma,* which is delight or pleasure. These last two are the natural drives of what Freud calls the id, namely the purely biological energy of the psyche: the power principle and the pleasure principle. In the Indian scheme, these id drives—*artha* and *kāma*—are to be realized under the ceiling of the *dharma,* which Freud would term the superego. In other words, "I want" is seen to be always subservient to "thou shalt." There is no mediation by the ego. These forces—the "I want" of the id and the "thou shalt" of the superego—are what I would call the motives of the nursery. There is no development in this scheme of what we would call the individual at all; there is no provision made for what Freud calls ego development. The ego principle, which relates the subconscious desires of the id and the social demands of *dharma,* the superego—this "I" is contaminated by and totally identified with the id principle according to this system. They cohere. In the Orient, "I" equals "I want."

In our Western view, as laid out by Jung and Freud, we differentiate between id and ego. Ego is the principle that links you, this individual, here and now—a set of subconscious desires and needs—to this situation, here and now—a universe of social and environmental phenomena. You are not to think in terms of stereotypes or clichés. You are not to think that this situation ever happened before. It didn't. It is absolutely unique. Its demands are absolutely unique. The decision has to be made now.

Furthermore, as a result of assuming an ego, you assume responsibility for what you do; this concept of the ego as responsible, that too is missing in the Orient. What you do in the Orient is what you do as a soldier. A soldier is not personally responsible for anything that he does under command. He does it because that is the order and he is simply a good soldier. Similarly, if you are acting according to *dharma,* doing just what you are told, there is no personal responsibility on you at all. You do not assume responsibility for anything.

Now, the fourth aim of life, according to Hinduism—the one that carries people out of society, into the forest and beyond—is release, *mokṣa.* We will touch on that later.

In the West, the fundamental principle is the Protestant idea of the individual deciding the nature of God's message through the filter of his or her own conscience. It has to do with an idea of freedom of will, freedom of conscience, freedom of decision, assumption of personal responsibility; there is none of this in the Orient at all.

Agents of the Eternal

Let me draw once again a distinction between what we used to think of as the Orient, the Near East from which the biblical tradition comes, and the other Orients of India and the Far East. I have spoken of the great mathematical cycles of the eons. The image, the mythological image, that is used to describe the coming of the end and then the return is the image of the deluge, the flood. The world sinks in the primordial waters again, into the primordial abyss, and then it comes out in form and then it goes back and then it comes out. This happens automatically, mathematically.

In Mesopotamia, about 2500 B.C.—the same time as the settlement of the Indus Valley—a new version of the deluge appears in the Sumerian texts. The idea now is that God sends the deluge in punishment for man's sins. This is a totally different flood. In this case you do not have the automatic, impersonal coming and going. You have the punishment of someone who is guilty. There are enormous implications in this shift of action. In the first place, a certain sense of wonder and magnitude and glory is lost. There is no question about it: the old cycle of flood and return, flood and return is a great, magnificent, wondrous affair, the blooming of a cosmic being of which we are but morsels. The Near Eastern model, which comes down to us in the story of Noah, throws man into a personal relationship to a deity who has free will.

The deities in India and the Far East are agents of the eternal cycle. For the most part they are, as it were, executives, performing the necessary acts, bringing about the inevitable processes of the cosmic cycle like roosters crowing to raise the Sun.

However, when you have the deity himself making the laws, himself sending the flood, then you have a quite different principle in play. And it is at about this time that an enormous shift takes place in the whole consciousness of the world west of Iran. No longer do we think of god and man as mere aspects of a total being that is the cosmos; God and man become separate from each other and in tension with each other and God is judging man and acting upon him. Furthermore, God sits, as it were, *behind* the laws of the universe, not in front of them.

In the older system of the great mathematics of the cosmos, the gods are, as I say, simply the executives, and you have the great natural laws that govern everything. But when you have a god who determines what the laws are to be, who says, "Let it be so," and it is so, then you have a stress on the personality that doesn't exist east of Mesopotamia.

This puts the Near East into a rather close relationship to the individualism of the West that I have been talking about. However, there is a great distinction to be made. In the Levant, the stress is always on obeying. The idea is that God has given a revelation that is encompassed in a book, in a statement. This goes for Zoroastrianism, for Judaism, for Christianity, for Islam—all of the biblical religions out of the Near East. In each case, there is a book, a revealed truth, and one does not quibble with that. One finds out what it says, and the one who does quibble with that is by definition an evil person, a person who has lost touch with the truth and is an outcast, a heretic. Whole races, whole worlds can fall away.

In fact the usual pattern in the Near East is that there is the word, and it has been passed down through one true tradition to the people. In this part of the world, the typical hero is not the individual nor is it the reincarnating monad: it is the tribe or, with the later world religions such as Christianity and Islam, the church that carries the truth. The individual is, as it were, an organ of that organism. The Christian is one with all Christians in the organism of Christ—that is, the Church. In the Hebrew mythos, you have the seed of Abraham, the Chosen People, who will be vindicated at the end of time. In Islam the relationship is through the word, through the Koran.

In each case, the individual relationship to the god is through the community; it is not a personal one. There must be ten people present for a Jewish service to take place—this is the idea of the minyan. Likewise, in the Catholic Church, salvation can only be achieved through the sacraments, most of which must be administered by a priest.

So there is this idea of the Fall and a process of the whole community to connect back to God. The individual participates in that, but only as a foot soldier, as it were.

The interesting thing in Europe is that this Levantine idea comes into contact and conflict with the Western concept of the individual. You can see it happening in the early Christian community, the attempt to fuse the two ideas of the individual and the community. And I would say that you can see the joint in the Christian notion of two judgments, the personal judgment and the general judgment. Each of us at death is judged—that is the individual problem. Then, at the end of the world, there is a final judgment where everybody comes back for a grand second hearing. It is only then that the world ends. Here we have the two traditions brought together.

In Europe I would say we have a very strong individualistic tradition that goes back certainly to the Greeks and is to be identified also in the north European pagan traditions of the Celts and the Germans. In the Middle Ages, this tradition comes into contact with the idea of the community, the Chosen People, the group outside of which there is no salvation. The statement made by David Ben-Gurion, Israel's first president, comes out of this tradition: "A Jew who does not live in Israel lives in sin." Just so Pope Boniface VIII stated in a papal bull the dogma, *"Extra ecclesiam nula salus"*—no salvation outside the church! This is an old traditional idea that comes entirely out of the Near East—those who do not reside or pray within the sacred confines are said to have no god. There you have the idea of the community as hero, the people of God.

In the further East the great hero is neither the individual nor the people. Rather it is the *jīva,* the reincarnating monad. "The Humbling of Indra" illustrates this idea perfectly:

Indra is the king of the gods. He has followed his *dharma.* He has pursued *artha,* destroying the great monster Vṛtra. He has indulged in *kāma,* ordering the construction of his stately pleasure dome.

Then Viṣṇu and Śiva come to visit, and in a moment of illumination, all of Indra's virtue, success, and pleasure turn to ash; he is ready to chuck it all in and move on to the next game.

The big collision in the Orient is between those three ends that I have already mentioned—virtue, pleasure, success—and the fourth end, which is called *mokṣa,* release. Indra concedes all of the worldly drives and starts to pursue the final end, throwing it all off, letting it all drop away. Now this is not individuation in Jung's terms at all. It is canceling everything, even ego. It is canceling desire for pleasure. It is canceling desire for success. It is canceling even the pursuit of virtue.

Well, when Indra's beautiful queen, Indrani, learns that her spouse—her prime divinity, you might say—is about to go off to the forest, she realizes that she too has to pursue *dharma.* Indra has not fulfilled his duty; the world still needs a king; she still needs a husband. So she sets Bṛhaspati the priest to fetch her husband back from the brink.

In this story I think we can see all of the Oriental possibilities at play. You can see the force of the idea of the reincarnation of the *jīva,* the force of the egolessness idea, the force of the vast development of cosmic eons in which the individual plays simply an ephemeral function. You can see also that two ways are indicated: the way of quitting and the way of coming back.

The Imagery of Rebirth Yoga[38]

The Journey to the Sun's Door

When a tradition, such as ours, is failing to get its message across—when its mythology is no longer fully functional—terrible things can begin to happen. The mythic structure of the society no longer supports the psychological development of the individual. In discussing psychosis, I took the phenomenology of schizophrenia as an example. With the schizophrenic, you have a person drowning, so to say, in the ocean of the imagery of the instinct system.

Let us talk about the miracle of the person who knows how to swim in this ocean, someone who can navigate across this night sea and emerge on the other shore, reborn from the sea.

Let us remember that when we come to the question of rebirth, there are two main orders. The first is this miracle of rebirth in time, which is symbolized by the Moon that dies and is resurrected. The Moon sheds its shadow as a serpent sheds its skin, and so the serpent plays the role also as a symbol of this same principle of the life that is reborn from its own death. And, as we have seen, the horns of the Moon are frequently associated with the horns of the bull. And so the bull in traditional mythology also is associated with this symbology of death and rebirth. The sacrifice of the bull is symbolic of the sacrifice of that mortal part in us which leads to the release of the eternal.

The other idea of rebirth is that of not coming back at all, not being reborn here, but passing beyond the spheres of rebirth altogether to a transcendent light. And the typical image for this is the Sun. The Sun is all light. The Moon carries darkness within it, but wherever the Sun goes, there is no darkness; there are only the shadows of those forces that do not open to its light. And so the image of the Sun door speaks of another time of rebirth: the return of the lost one, the one lost in the sphere of shadows and time to that eternal root that is his own great root.

The animal symbolic of this Sun principle, as the bull is symbolic of the Moon, is the lion with his great, radiant solar face. And as the Sun rising quenches the Moon and quenches the stars, so the lion roar sends the grazing animals scattering. And the lion pouncing on the bull, which is a motif that you will see in primitive and ancient art, particularly in the Middle East and Persia, is symbolic of this business of the Sun rising and quenching the Moon. In contrast to the serpent, we have the eagle, which is the solar bird. And so we have these parallels: eagle against serpent, lion against bull, Sun against Moon.

The great figures of the early mythologies of the vegetal rebirth of life every year, coming back, coming back—such figures as Tammuz, Adonis, and Osiris—are associated closely with the bull.

But when we come to a figure like the Buddha, who represents the transcendence of all reincarnation whatsoever, we have the lion symbol. And if you look at the Buddha thrones in the art of India, you will see it is a lion's throne. And the Buddha's message is said to be the lion roar. What I want to talk about now is how to learn to roar like a lion.

The first aphorism of the Yoga Sūtra is, as we have seen, that yoga is the intentional stopping of the spontaneous activity of the mind. We see each other here, in the plane of *māyā,* because there is an echo in this substance in our minds that takes the forms of what we see and hear as well. And when you move your eyes quickly, you can see how rapidly this substance changes form. When our mind is in movement, like the rippling surface of a pond, all that we see are broken images. But let the wind be still, and the water cleared of all sediment, and you will see perfectly reflected the forms that formerly had been only broken in your experience. And so it is when the mind is stilled in yoga: all these broken reflections that we are, are gathered back to the image of which we are the broken reflections. And one sees not only the reflected sky but also down into the water depth, down into the water depth of one's own being, and the image beheld then is the form of forms, that form which in all of us is broken.

When this is experienced, the fascination is completely absorbing. And it may be such that the one who beholds it would not wish to return to see the broken forms again—then he remains in that fixed contemplation, and as they say, the body drops off. He has been returned to union with that which he indeed is. That which we call our ego, that which we think of as ourselves, is but the broken reflection of that which is our true self. And the discovery of that true self is the recovery of union with our own being.

Aum is the sound value of that union. We remember that the first sound in *aum,* "a," is associated with what is called "waking consciousness." That is the state of most of us throughout our lives. When consciousness is awake, what one sees seems to be separate from oneself—subject and object are separate from each other. On this level, Aristotelian logic prevails: *a* is not *b.* "U" is associated with dream consciousness. When you move into the level of dream consciousness, all the laws of logic change. There, although you think you are seeing something that is not you, it is actually you that you are seeing, because the dream is simply a manifestation of your own will and energy—you created the dream and yet you are surprised by it. So the duality there is illusory. There, subject and object, though apparently separate, are the same.

The realms of the gods and demons—heaven, purgatory, hell—are of the substance of dreams. Myth, in this view, is the dream of the world. If we accept gods as objective realities, then they are the counterpart of your dream—this is a very important point—dream and myth are of the same logic. This is a point that we are getting in our modern psychology, both in the pioneering work of Freud and Jung and in contemporary writers such as Eric Fromm. And since the subject and object seem to be separate but are not separate in the dream, so the god that seems to be outside of you in myth (or religion, if you prefer) is not different from you. You and your god are one. Now we are moving to something very interesting. All the heavens and gods are within you and are identical with aspects of your own consciousness on the dream level.

The final audible sound in *aum,* "m," brings us to the level of deep, dreamless sleep. Here, consciousness has been covered over by ignorance, by darkness. This is the realm out of which consciousness then will reappear. But the fact that we are not conscious of it does not mean that it is not there. But it is not consciousness of anything; there are no differentiated things. It is called an "undifferentiated mass" of consciousness.

The goal of the various forms of yoga is to go into that realm of undifferentiated consciousness *while remaining awake.* We don't have a counterpart to this concept in our Western vocabularies. It doesn't even have a name in India; it is called simply the fourth state, and that is the fourth letter of the syllable, the level of silence. Because all the words that we speak refer either to waking images and logic, dream images and logic, or ignorance. We do not have words for this, and so it is the ultimate silence, but it is that which we are.

The whole aim of Oriental religions, in contrast to ours, is to bring about in us an experience of our identity with that void which is no void, what the Buddhists call *śūnyatā.* It is beyond all description. That which is true being and mystery of all things is beyond naming, beyond imaging. So that any name or image that pretends to be the name or image of the ultimate divine thing is a false name and image; it is a mere idol. The goal of these religions is to help us realize that that being which is transcendent of definition is our own being.

You can take anything and regard it in that dimension of its mystery. You can take any object, put a ring around it, and regard it not in its system of relationships as serving a purpose, as made of certain substances, but just in its mystery as being; the mystery of the being of this book in your hands is identical with the mystery of the being of the universe. So any stick or stone can be taken as a basis for mystery, for contemplation. The goal then of these religions is to bring about a realization of this identity of yourself with that which comes as an experience.

Of course, our religions do not strive for the experience of identity with the ultimate divine; in fact, that experience is the prime heresy in the West. Our religions intend to create a relationship, the relationship of that which is not God to God. And this relationship is achieved through participation in what is taken to be God's chosen society, or the founded church. In the Christian tradition, Christ is true God and true Man; we relate to him as man, and he thereby brings us into relationship with God the Father.

In the East, everybody is true God and true Man. And the whole goal of the religion is to realize that divinity in yourself. So here we have an intention that is very different from anything we conceive of in our religious traditions. When you have heard the sound of God, this sound of the divine in all things, it is absolutely everywhere—you are fascinated by that. And this properly, in the Orient, is the sphere of art. It is the rendition of that sound, that radiance, through whatever is contemplated. That is what Oriental art is about, to bring about the perception of the transcendent in all things.

In the *kuṇḍalinī* yoga, this realization corresponds to the point between the eyes, *ājñā*. The soul beholds the beatific vision of the energy in full radiance. This is the vision that I spoke of when the water stands still, the form of forms beheld.

The Indian word for this form of forms is *īśvara,* "lord." Any god can be taken as this lord. The image that you have held in your mind as the image of God is what will there be experienced, be it Yahweh, Śiva, Viṣṇu, or the Goddess, be it Christ or the Trinity or the highest image of the Buddha. Any will be all right. And what beholds it is that *jīva* that has gone through many incarnations and is the soul of your own existence. Here, the subject beholds its proper object. At this level the erotic principle of the second *cakra* finds its goal: the true beloved, the beloved that our soul intends, is God. And anything short of that is simply an inkling of what the experience of God would be.

Now, says Ramakrishna, speaking of this, we're only at the sixth *cakra* and we are in heaven now. Well, we might ask, what more do you want? The *jīva* at this level beholds, however, an image that has characteristics, qualities. This can't be the whole thing. Furthermore we are separate from it; we have not experienced identity with it. And so there comes the effort for the final realizations.

In this thinking, heaven is the last and final temptation. The Yoga Sūtra says when the *kuṇḍalinī* has reached this level, beholding the divine, and the divine landscape of the heavens with the holy sages and saints and all, if he so much as thinks, I have made it, I am here, this is my bliss, he goes right down the scale again, because ego has been enforced.

Ramakrishna said that the experience is as though you were to see a light through a pane of glass. It is, as al-Hallaj told us, the agony of the moth that is trying to reach the flame and only bangs against the glass. He wants to reach the flame and become the flame and burn away his separate entity by union with the flame—that is the goal of the mystic. And so you withdraw the pane of glass, and both are gone. There is no God, there is no one to behold; there is no subject, there is no object. We are in the realm of transcendent silence. This is the ultimate goal of all Oriental intention.

Now we come to a very strange mystery. What is it that happens as you pass from *ājñā,* the center of command, where the serpent power reaches the highest level within the realm of manifestation, to *sahasrāra,* the thousand-petaled lotus at the crown of creation?

What can we say of this strange thing that happens between here and here, so that here there is nothing? You cannot say a thing either is or is not. The things are no things, there is nothing there. Here, below, all things dual. This line is the mystery of *māyā.* The word *māyā* comes from a root *mā,* which means "to measure forth; to build." *Māyā* is what builds forth the world.

Remember that *māyā* has three powers. The first power is called the "obscuring power," which obscures the radiance of the ultimate. The second power is called the "projecting power," which projects the world of broken forms. The third power is said to be the "revealing power," which is the power rendered in art, when through the forms we experience the radiance.

You can perceive exactly the same things either in their obscuring or in their revealing aspect, depending on how far your levels of perception have risen. When you are studying things in the spirit of the first three *cakras,* the obscuring power is working. But when the radiance is experienced in art, the fascination of the art object is that of discovering your own true radiance there, because there is only one radiance, and that is the radiance of full consciousness. Then you have the awakening, so to say, to full realization.

In these images, these themes are translated into mythological images. The upper ultimate light may be depicted as the father. Then, along this line, *māyā* becomes the mother, through whom the energy of the father becomes incarnate. That is the imagery, for instance, of God the Father, Mary, and God the Son, and the Holy Ghost representing the actual energy that is transformed from Father to Son through the Virgin.

That is the role played by the Indian goddess Kālī. She, in her role of projecting power, is the one who projects all forms into being. She, in her role as the revealing power, is rendered in the form of a horrendous destroyer: she destroys the self-existence of things and unites them to their source. She is black as night because she is that mother-void out of which all things come and back to which they go.

This mystery may also be depicted in the aspect of Śiva, particularly in his dancing form as Naṭarāja. He is shown with the upper right hand holding a little hourglass-shaped drum. That drum going *tick-tick-tick* is the veil of time, which shuts out the dimension of eternity. Eternity is not a long time; eternity has nothing to do with time. Time-thinking is that which shuts out the eternity dimension. So when you think, Shall I be alive after death, you are thinking in temporal terms. That is the kind of thinking that belongs to lunar consciousness.

Figure 9. Śiva Naṭarāja

When you realize, however, that eternity is right here, now, and that it is possible to experience the eternity of your own truth and being, here, now, so that that which you are was never born and will never die—then you are thinking and experiencing in terms of the solar mystery, the solar life. So this little hourglass shuts us away from eternity by bringing about the creation of the world of time and ourselves within it. The upper left hand of the god holds a flame, the flame of illumination, the solar flame that burns away the veil of time. On the right, we have the hand of creation, on the left the hand of destruction. One hand brings you into the sphere of illusion, while the other hand opens your consciousness.

The lower right hand is held up in a gesture, or *mūdra,* that says, "Don't be afraid." Meanwhile, the lower left hand is in the *mūdra* that is called the elephant or teaching posture; where the elephant has gone through the jungle, all animals can follow. Where the great teacher has gone, all the disciples can follow. So what does that hand do? It points to the left foot, which is lifted, and that foot means "release," whereas the right foot drives down onto the back of a little dwarf, whose name is Ignorance. The right foot drives us all into this realm of ignorance, the left releases. Creation, destruction—don't be afraid because, though there is incarnation in ignorance, there is release.

In the midst of this dance, Śiva's head is perfectly still; this is called "the drop," the *bindu,* that point through which eternity breaks. His right ear has a man's earring; his left a woman's. This is the sphere where the pairs of opposites come forth. In the hair, there is a skull, meaning death, and there is a Moon, meaning rebirth. And there is a little female form that represents the River Ganges, which carries the grace of the heavenly knowledge and experience into the world of being.

The whole figure is surrounded by a great aureole of flame. This is the dancing god that fills the entire universe and dances in every atom and in every cell of your body. And you are that Śiva—that is the ultimate statement: *Śivo'ham*—"I am that Śiva."

Hearing the Intermediate State: The Tibetan Book of the Dead

I have spoken about the symbolism of rebirth in Hindu terms; now I want to explore it in Buddhist terms. The great text for this exploration is the

Bardo Thödol, "Hearing in the Intermediate State," or *The Tibetan Book of the Dead,* as it was translated by W. Y. Evans-Wentz and Lāma Kazi Dawa-Samdup.[39] This translation has a pair of very fine introductions, one by Evans-Wentz and the other by Sir John Woodruff, who is one of the greatest English explicators of the Tantric systems. There is also a commentary by Jung, who points out the relationship of all these symbols to our Western psychology. It is a marvelous, rich, very wonderful book.

The Bardo Thödol is the product of the highly esoteric Tibetan Vajrayāna school of Buddhism. This book tells about the forty-nine days that elapse between death and rebirth. The goal, however, is *not* to be reborn, so that if you can stop the descent to rebirth, well and good.

Beside you, as you lie dying, will be your chaplain, or *lāma,* who has been your spiritual guide. And he will tell you where you are on this mythological journey into the realm beyond the realms of waking and dream consciousness—beyond waking, it's really mostly dream consciousness that you are in. The notion is that at the moment of death, you behold the void and the radiance that are the light. If you are not ready, however, you can't hold to it. It is terrifying, because you want to hold to your own personality, and it blasts you and you are returned to the round of rebirth.

So the *lāma* will be saying, as the last breath is breathed, "You are now before the Light, try to hold to it. I have taught you how to do it, now go to work and hang on." This is the passage to the seventh *cakra,* the top. If you fail here, you come down to the level of the sixth *cakra,* the level of the radiant, beneficent aspects of the divine. And in the Buddhist system, these will be represented as the five *dhyāni* Buddhas. The first is called Vairocana; it is a Buddha holding the thunderbolt that symbolizes illumination. Next we come to the Buddhas of the East, of the South, of the West, and of the North. And then to all five of these Buddhas together in the form of a great circle with Vairocana in the center. The Buddha of the East is called Akśobhya, the one who supports the thunderbolt, and he represents the integrity of the illuminating experience. The Buddha of the South is called Ratnasambhava, the one born of a jewel, and he represents the radiance of beauty of illumination. And the Buddha of the West is Amitābha, the Buddha of inexhaustible radiance, and he is the great Buddha of love and compassion. And the Buddha then of the North is called Amoghasiddhi, and he represents the Buddha of directed effort. Each of these has a color associated with him: blue in the East, yellow in the South, red in the West, green in the North. They will attempt to help you to release yourself from the fear and desire that are drawing you back from union with the Buddha mind.

Sometimes, you will see these represented in a simple *maṇḍala*—this is simply the Sanskrit word meaning "circle"—with the four colors round about and the white of Vairocana in the center.

The whole idea of these *maṇḍalas* is to relate each of the parts to the center, to the whole. The idea is that when you contemplate such an image, you are harmonized inside.

Jung found that he could help harmonize the psyches of his patients by having them draw *maṇḍalas.* Each of us has disparate interests, disparate ideas, conflicting purposes, and conflicting ideals. And if you can put one of your purposes, let's say in the north, and the opposite purpose in the south, and then others in the east and west, you sort of pull yourself together, and your mind will in its dreams begin to suggest ways to harmonize the different thrusts of your life.

And so that is the way these things function: the religious symbols are harmonizing powers. That's the whole sense of mythology, to help you to harmonize your individual life with the general life, the life of the society and of the universe.

If you still haven't been able to release yourself from the fall, you come to the stage then of the fifth-*cakra* Buddhas, and these are horrendous.

When you see the *thaṇkas,* those long Buddhist pictures from Tibet, you'll see many horrendous-looking figures with great swords and terrifying faces, often with many faces, standing on great monsters and holding many weapons in their many hands and embracing their consorts, because the male and female principles always work together there. There is no notion of God or anything like that as being exclusively male, as we have in our somewhat patriarchically prejudiced tradition. Here the two principles work together. And these horrendous figures are the ones who are smashing our hold on ourselves.

The beneficent ones would have released us if we could have let go; but we haven't let go, so now comes real force. The thing to realize, however, is that these horrendous ones are the same as the beneficent ones, only in more brutal aspect, because we have been brutal in holding on to ourselves. And again, we get the five in the regular series going on down. On this level, there's an interesting point: they represent vices, the vice of egoism, the vice of pride. But the vice of pride is simply the negative aspect of the virtue of beauty. The vice of lust is the negative aspect of the virtue of compassion. The vice of jealousy is simply the negative aspect of the virtue of directed intention or effort. And so by carrying through our vices, we can achieve redemption. The *lāma* will say, "Remember that these are simply forms of your own mind consciousness."

If, once again, we are unable to let go, we come to the crisis: we are getting pretty dangerously close to rebirth now. We have come to the fourth *cakra,* and this is the *cakra* of judgment. As you remember, this is where the devotee touched the feet of God, and now he may lose the feet. It seems to me that this is where our college campuses are poised—between the realms of contemplation and the realms of what is now being advertised as activism. The whole thing will be lost if you respond to what are called the "karmic winds," these blowing breaths of action that cry, "Kill, kill!" There is something to be gained; there is something to be lost.

You have to hold to the thought that there is nothing to hold, nothing to gain, nothing to do. If you lose that, there will build up behind you a wall of three powers, and then you cannot go back. And the three powers are stupidity, malice or anger, and desire or lust. Those are the powers that move the world.

At this point, the Lord of Judgment appears in the form of a great ox with many hands—this is a figure you see all through the Tibetan tradition. And his minions will come and you will find yourself carved to pieces, your guts torn out, all the tortures you can possibly think of in the Orient—and there is quite a little glossary of tortures—will be enacted upon you. At this point, you have to think, These are simply manifestations of my own thought.

If you can't think that, you start for the finale. At this point, Freudian psychology reappears. The soul in the descent, at the second *cakra* level, begins to see males and females copulating. The *lāma* is saying, "Try not to get between them." And if that is lost, then comes this very interesting experience of delight in what's about to happen. If you are to be born now as a male, you will find yourself loving your mother and hating your father.

And if you are going to be born as a female, you will find yourself hating your potential mother and loving your father. Did Freud teach us anything?

After all this, having gone for forty-nine days through all the plagues and the supreme consciousness down to this, this little squealing thing is born and thinks it has come new into the world. But within it is the whole thing again; the soul has come back again.

This is the Oriental concept now that underlies the cults that we see. This is the aim: to find that in yourself.

If that is achieved, if one manages to reach undifferentiated consciousness while awake, then there are two responses. Suppose that you have found the light and have contemplated this still pond. You may let the body drop off, close the eyes, as it were, and unite with this central transcendent realization. Or you may open the eyes and take delight in the play of forms, seeing through them the one form. That is the attitude of world affirmation, the affirmation of every single thing, even the monsters.

When I was in India, I listened around awhile to see who the wise man would be that I would choose to have my principal mystical discussion with. And I chose one who lived in the world, eyes open.

His name was Sri Krishna Menon.[40] He had been a policeman, not a very highly regarded profession in India, and he was, nevertheless, a great saint. I was introduced to him and went into the room where he was sitting, and there was a chair for me to sit in, so I sat. We greeted each other respectfully, and he asked, "Do you have a question?" Then I had the good fortune to ask him the question that he had asked his guru when he first came to him. And so we had a fine conversation.

What I asked him was, "If, as we know, all things are *Brahman,* are this divine energy, then why do we renounce the world, why do we renounce vice, why do we renounce stupidity? Why do we not see the divine shining through the most brutal, the most horrendous, the most stupid, and most dark?"

He responded, "For you and me, that is where it is."

Creativity in Oriental Myth[41]

Avatars of Light: Indian Art

In the classical textbooks on literary techniques in India, four types of subjects are indicated as proper objects for the artist's attention: first, abstract qualities such as goodness, truth, beauty; second, types of action and moods, such as slaying monsters, or slaying an enemy, pursuing a lover, or moods of melancholy and bliss and so forth; third, types of human being—*brahmins, kṣatriyas,* merchants, lovers, and so forth; and finally deities. All of these, you will observe, are abstract. There is no interest in the individual as such, as a unique, distinct phenomenon. When one looks at the glorious panorama of Indian art, one sees a repetition of themes—beautiful themes, dependable themes, motifs that recur time and time again. And if you compare that galaxy of forms with their counterparts in post-Renaissance Europe, you will be struck by the absence of individual inflection in any of these works.

Consider the works of a Michelangelo or Leonardo—the time and concern that they spent on rendering what we call character, personality, the individual entity in such a way that one realizes this is a unique thing. This is altogether antagonistic to the spirit of Oriental art. This stress on the individual as a unique phenomenon to be cultivated in his idiosyncrasies and brought to flower, so to say, as something that never existed before; the sense, too, on the part of the individual of personal responsibilities for something—this development of what may be called the individual or the ego is totally alien to the spirit of Oriental thought and the arts. The Oriental artist not only must be concerned with types when he renders forms but also he must himself seek no such thing as self-expression. The idea of inventive creativity, the idea of self-expression that we hear so much about when we speak with our artists, the artist's agony finding his own special language, his own special message—all of these terms that are so common in our aesthetic discourse are not only alien but also completely antithetical to the Oriental spirit.

They are alien, too, of course, to Oriental religiosity, which is concerned precisely with the quenching of ego, the quenching of the individual, and the evanescence of this passing moment, which is merely *ahaṃ,* "I." This emphasis on types does tend sometimes to bring out the inferior side of Oriental art: a rather dry, academic repetition, a recurrence of mere stereotypes, rather than evocation of archetypes. I don't want to speak about the negative side of the subject, however. What I want to speak about is the wonderful mystery and technique for the rendering of the immortal in all things. This is the wonderful song that one hears when one reads the Bhagavad Gītā or any of the great texts of Eastern philosophy. This is the song of that immortal spirit that never was born and never dies but is born in all things, lives in all things, and dies in all things, and the radiance of which gives things their glory. This is the song of *Brahman,* which is sung in Indian art itself and in Oriental art in general. It is to that song, that impulse, that I want to speak somewhat.

The Indian artist is a sort of yogi. (I will examine East Asian artists in a moment.) After he has learned the physical techniques, the manual techniques of his craft; after he has performed the assignments assigned to him by his master and done the craftsmanly work that was his to do and becomes himself a master craftsman and receives the commission to erect a temple or to design the sculpture decor that will then be executed by his craftsmen, he must meditate in order to bring before his own spirit, his own inner eye, the vision of the deity whom he is to render. It's wonderful to read of the origins of many Oriental temples—of many Oriental cities, even; how a great monarch, a holy monarch, had a dream, a vision, and in this he saw the city. I think that this is why when one goes to some of these great Asian cities even today, one feels that one is moving in a dreamworld. The city is dreamlike in its conception and very frequently was actually conceived in a dream. This dream was then rendered as far as possible in stone and brick.

Figure 10. Benares along the Ganges

The artist proposing to depict a certain divinity—let us say Viṣṇu—must first study all the texts. Of course, he knows them already from his apprenticeship, but he reviews them to learn what precisely the traits, the signs and symbology of this deity are. Then he must compose his mind and pronounce in his spirit the deity's seed syllable; that is to say he must pronounce the sound that is the verbal counterpart of the deity's image. Then, if he has the fortune to receive the grace of the god's manifestation, the deity will appear in his mind in his radiant form and this then is the model. At their best, the works of Indian art are literal renditions of visions, and they have this visionary, dreamlike quality as well as a wonderful vigor and power in physical strength.

Figure 11. Viṣṇu sheltered by cosmic serpent Ananta, c. eighteenth century A.D.

Briefly, what is art in this view? Art is an arrangement of forms that will show that divine presence which is in all things through themselves. The radiance of art, the fascination of art, is the radiance and fascination of self-recognition in other; and that self is not the self of ego, not the one "I" who is seen, but it is that inhabiting *ātman-Brahman* that inhabits all things. It is that self which in sound is *aum*—all music is *aum,* and all things are *Brahman.* Oriental art then is the showing of the divinity of things that you are looking at, and that divinity is not, from the Oriental standpoint, the unique but the general.

As you may remember, in the *kuṇḍalīni* yoga, *aum* is first heard at the fourth *cakra.* I must say, the passage of the *kuṇḍalīni* seems to throw a very vivid light on the aim and techniques of Eastern art. Indian art in particular deals with the progression from the fourth and the sixth *cakra,* where you are either beholding the things of the world and experiencing the divine radiance through them, or you are beholding the divine being itself. Now it is characteristic of Indian art that its stress is on divine beings;

Indian art is a depiction largely of divinities. You can go through the great books of pictures of Indian art and you'll see one after another of these great divinities. And when one looks at the Indian temples, there is something quite extraordinary about them. They burst into the landscape—they are not part of the landscape, they burst into the land, as it were, from a superior realm. These wonderful caves that are carved right into the rocks; as you move into them, you have moved out of the world of two-eyed optical experience into the world of transcendent manifestation. Indian art in general then is an art concerned with elimination of the normal two-eyed experience of the world; opening as it were this third eye in the middle and seeing the vision of eternity, and it is a kind of vision of heaven.

Figure 12. The Descent of the Ganges

Light and Dark: East Asian Art

This is rather different I think in feeling from the art that one perceives when one turns to the Far East, to China or Japan. Buddhism went to the Far East from India, and it brought along with it this wonderful art depicting heaven, depicting the divinities of the upper world. The natural tendency of the Far Eastern mind, however, is much more earthy, much more matter-of-fact, much more devoted to things, to the material world. As Dr. Suzuki once pointed out, whereas in India the term meaning myriads translates into English as "innumerable"—this term occurs many times in Sanskrit indicating the number of years that elapse in the course of an eon and so forth—in China the word for all the things in the world is ten thousand things. In India you have myriads and myriads and myriads and dreams and dreams and dreams; in China and Japan they speak of the *ten thousand things,* the things right here and now; that is what they are concerned with. So I would say that in general there is a sort of shift of emphasis from what may be called the sixth *cakra,* from the place where God is seen in his purity or where the deities appear as in an epiphany, to the fourth *cakra;* to this beautiful world, this world of nature and of man, where one is concerned with the idiosyncrasies of this, that, or another apparition always as manifesting this wonderful glory of the eternal principle.

There are two great art forms that we can recognize in the Far East. The first is the art of the Buddhist images and other divine representations; this is art created in the spirit of the Hindu visionary world that we have been talking about. But the art of the Chinese and Japanese landscape—those beautiful kakemonos of the countryside—has a quite different spirit.

Behind this art lies a philosophy that is native to the Far East. This is the philosophy expressed in Chinese Taoism. Tao means, as we know, "the way." This is the way of nature. The way of nature is the way in which dark and light interplay. There are two principles that combine in various modulations to constitute the world and its way, and these principles respectively are the *yang* and the *yin.* These words are sometimes translated as the male and female principles, respectively, but that is not their primary meaning. Yang and yin in their origin refer to the sunny and shady side of a stream; the yang is the sunny side, and the yin is the shady side. What is the situation on the sunny side? It is light, it is hot, and the heat of the Sun is dry. In the shade, on the other side, you have the Earth; it is cold without the Sun on it, and it is moist within. Moist, cold, and dark, and hot, dry, and light play in counteraction. Earth and Sun are associated respectively with the feminine and masculine principles and with the passive and the active principles. This is a very profound symbol.

There is no moral imperative here; this is not the battle of the sons of light and the sons of darkness that underlies Zoroastrianism and the biblical traditions. Light is not better or stronger than dark, nor is dark better or stronger than light. They are simply the two balanced principles on which the world rests: the light and the dark.

Figure 13. "Taking a lute to visit a friend," attributed to Jiang Song, c. 1500 A.D.

As I look out my window, I see light and dark, light and dark; wherever we look that is what we see. An artist can take a brush and put black on white and bring forth all of the inflections of the natural world. By using light and dark, he depicts the forms, which in their very essence are composed of light and dark. This is a wonderful thing. The outer form of light and dark is a manifestation of what is within. So the artist with his brush is manipulating the very principles that underlie the whole of nature, and the artwork brings out, as it were, the very essence of the world itself and that essence is the interplay of these two in many modulations. The delight of seeing this interplay is the delight of the man who does not wish to break through the walls of the universe but wishes to stay in the world playing with the song and inflection of this great duad, yang and yin.

In order to experience what is before him, the artist has to look, and looking is a passive, yin activity. One can't look harder; you can't say to your eyes, "See more!" You look and the world comes to you. There is a wonderful word to express this state, *wuwei,* which means "nonaction." It doesn't mean not doing anything; it means not forcing anything, so that the thing will open up. Just as the divinity showed himself to the meditating Hindu, so does the world show itself in its form to the contemplative eye of the Far Eastern artist. In East Asia, we find the notion of the world coming into form with a spontaneity of its own, which is the spontaneity of the nature of the artist himself, and then the spontaneity of the brush as it renders this. Not anything programmed, not anything planned—this is the essential idea behind this Taoist view.

There are two words for law that are described by Joseph Needham and his wonderful second volume on *Science and Civilisation in China;* the word *li* and the word *tse.*[42] The word *li* refers to the markings on a piece of jade, the natural grain of life; this is natural law, the law intrinsic to the universe. *Tse,* on the other hand, refers to the markings that are made on a cauldron by a stylus, markings made by man. This word refers to the social laws that are made, contrived laws, as opposed to natural laws. *Tse,* the laws thought up by the mind, are contrasted with *li,* the laws experienced as the very pattern of nature. The function of art is to know the latter, the laws of nature, the patterns of nature, the way nature moves, and to know these, the artist cannot force any laws on nature. So the artist takes on the wonderful, sensitive task of coordinating his own concept of nature—his concept of what is to be done and the discipline of action that he has learned—with the given forms of nature. This is *wuwei,* the balance between doing and not doing that yields the perfect artwork.

I should say that this spirit of doing-through-not-doing inhabits all traditional action in the Far East. While I was in Japan, I saw some of the sumo wrestling, the wonderful crazy contest of those big fellows that is, it has been said, the survival of the fattest. Now these men spend most of their time during the course of a bout standing in a crouch looking at each other. They do this about four times, meanwhile the Japanese crowd is in ecstasy watching, and then *bam!* they grab each other, and one fellow is on the ground within five seconds. What are they doing during all this preliminary business? They're supposed to be finding that point of center and inaction out of which movement will come spontaneously, and the one who hasn't found that center is the one who hits the mat.

If you want to learn to be a fencer in Japan and go to a fencing master, he will probably just leave you around for a while washing the dishes and so forth, and every now and then, he will pop out from somewhere and hit you on the head. Then you begin to prepare for this, waiting for him to come from *here*—and he comes from *there*. After weeks of this sort of thing, you learn that it is best not to be prepared at all, because if you have a notion of where the next attack is going to come from, then you are focused in the wrong direction, because that is not where it comes from. You have got to be in a state of absolute centeredness and spontaneous response. That is the basic lesson of the art of fencing.

I heard a darling story of one kendo fencing master of this type who said to the boys that were with him, "Anyone who can catch me by surprise in any way whatsoever, I shall bow before him." Of course, days and days went on, they tried to trick the old boy, but nobody could catch him unawares. One day, he wanted some water to bathe his feet because he'd been out in the mud. This little ten-year-old boy brought the basin in for him to bathe his feet in, but the water was too warm, and the master said, "Bring it cooler." The little boy brings it steaming hot, and the master, without taking notice, puts his feet in the hot water, pulls them out—and then he gets down in a very deep bow before the little boy.

The sin of inadvertence, of not being alert, is the sin of missing the moment of life, and the whole art of nonaction-in-action is the art of perpetual alertness. So that you are experiencing life all the time; you don't have to do anything: it lives in you, it moves in you, it speaks itself.

In all of these Oriental societies—Indian, Chinese, or Japanese—art is not simply the art of the canvas or the brush or the sculpture. It is the art of *life*. Coomaraswamy points out, "In the traditional Orient the artist is not a special kind of man, but every man is a special kind of artist."[43] As you can see, this awareness of existence is the central principle, and all of the crafts, all of the actions of life are opportunities to experience this divine presence that is our life. The function of the artist is to render that experience in a particularly acute way for the senses. The Indian artist, and the Indian mind, as I have said, tend to go out of the world to behold the gods, up in the sixth *cakra.* The Chinese art of the Tao and the Japanese art of Zen tend to contemplate nature.

There is a tendency in the old Chinese traditional Taoist works of art and poetry to leave the city and go out into the country and be in the countryside away from people, alone with nature. But in Japan, as in England, there are so many people and so little room that you can't be alone with nature, you can't be alone anywhere; you climb a big mountain and there is a little party up there already, so there is no escape from society, there is no escape from man.

As you may know, the Japanese use Chinese characters, or ideograms, for some of the more complex concepts. So, the Chinese and Japanese signs for "freedom" (Japanese *jiyū;* Chinese *ziyou*) are both exactly the same. The Chinese sign really means "freedom away from society"—under the great vault of heaven, picking mushrooms on the misty mountaintop; no one knows where I am. But the Japanese interpretation of the word is "freedom in the context of society"—you stay within your given circumstances, within what is imposed upon you by the society, the rules of the social situation. Within this context you find your freedom, because you realize the very life that shines through nature also shines through man and society.

There is a curious and extremely interesting aspect of the Japanese language. There is a form of very polite discourse known as "play language" *(asobase kotoba),* where instead of saying, "I see that you have come to Tokyo," one says, "I see that you are playing at being in Tokyo." The idea is that people do what they do voluntarily, as one enters a game. Life is a game. This goes so far that, when using this very polite language, you wish to say, "I hear that your father has died," the way to say it is, "I understand that your father has played at dying."

I submit that this is a glorious approach to life. What has to be done you do with such a will that you play at it. This is what Nietzsche calls the love of life, *amor fati.* It is the point that Spengler makes when he quotes Seneca saying, "He who goes with fate the fates lead; he who resists fate the fates pull." You have got to go. So realize that in coming into life—and of course this underlies part of the Oriental notion of reincarnation anyhow—you wanted to come into life, otherwise you wouldn't have come. In coming into this world at this time, you wanted it at this time. It's a big, great thing you decided to do—don't lose your nerve. Go through and play the game.

I'm sure we have all played one game or another, so we all know that the games that are the most fun are the ones that are the hardest. The ones with the most complicated system of challenges are the ones that really hold you if you really want to play a game.

So it is that artists are not content with doing simple things in their art. They like the challenge, the difficult thing. Why write a limerick when you can write a sonnet?

This whole attitude is made quite vivid in Japan by the art that is implicit in such a thing as the tea ceremony. Japanese life is terribly formal; even walking into a room and out, you are bound to make ninety-three mistakes before you go in and out—you are a bull, a bore all the time. But to make it still more difficult, there is this exquisitely intricate business of the tea ceremony.

I knew one little old lady in Kyoto who has been studying tea ceremony for sixty years, and she has her tea lesson twice a week still and she always speaks with the *asobase kotoba* play language when she speaks. The little tea spoon that's used to take the tea out and put it in the bowl—if, when you put it down on the table, you put it a sixteenth of an inch wrong, oh, everybody knows. It is worse than going to meet the queen with your galoshes on; it has just got to be precisely on the mark, all the time. Now the thing is to perform this exquisitely difficult affair with ease, with grace, and carry on what would appear to be a casual conversation meanwhile. Watching her one day, I remembered when I was an athlete at Columbia on the track team. We used to wear sweat clothes when we practiced so that when we got in a race and took the sweats off, running would be easy; you would feel very light. So it is here: after the tea ceremony, life in Japan is easy.

This attitude, art as the game of life, or the game of life as itself a form of art, is a wonderful, vigorous, joyous approach to the problem of living in the world. It is quite in contrast with ours in the West, which is based on the notion of universal guilt—there was a Fall somewhere, you remember, and we're all in a mess as a consequence. The Oriental idea is that the world is God's play—it's a game He's playing, if we choose to imagine Him as a He. Of course people get hurt playing football, people fall off horses, people fall out of automobiles; there is no such thing as a game without somebody getting hurt. Even playing chess you can use up your eyes and brains. The fun of the game is that it's a risky one, in a way, and since this is the game that was designed for us, so here goes. Art then is, as it were, the culminating statement, the key statement of the essence of life as a game, as an act of play. This corresponds, finally, to go back to India again, with the Indian notion of the world as God's play. So there is a wonderful community here between all grades of life as art.

There is a story told of a young Chinese scholar named Chu who went with a friend for a walk in the mountains. He and his friend came to an old monastery, an old temple that had fallen down, and there were just a few walls standing. In this ruin there lived an old Buddhist monk, and this monk greeted the two young men when they arrived and he showed them the walls and ruins of the temple.

Up on one of the walls were the remains of a quite charming picture. The picture showed a little town, and standing at one of the streets was a girl with her hair down, meaning she was unmarried—a married woman would have had her hair bound up. Chu, looking at this, just fell in love with that girl there in the picture. He was utterly enchanted by her. Before he knew it, because of the power of the monk, he was in the picture, and there was the girl. She said, "Come in." So in he went, and they had a passionate love affair that lasted for several days.

Then her little friends, her companions, arrived and they said, "Oh! Oh! And your hair is still down, put your hair up." So she did. They continued to live this way in the village for a while.

Then one day a monstrous noise was heard outside and there were some official officers coming to scout out foreigners and aliens. There was a terrible commotion and the young girl said, "You had better hide, you had better hide, you had better hide, you had better run down here!" He started to run and hide and pretty soon he came out of the picture and he was standing right where he'd been before he went into the picture. His friend who had missed him was delighted to see his return, and then they turned and they looked at the picture and what do you know, the girl's hair was up.

Now I don't think I want to try to interpret this.

I thought I would conclude, instead, with a brief reference to Zen, which I know has become rather fashionable recently. The word *zen,* as you may realize, is a Japanese way of pronouncing a Chinese word, *ch'an.* And this Chinese word, *ch'an,* is a Chinese way of pronouncing a Sanskrit word, which is *dhyāna,* and *dhyāna* means "contemplation." Contemplation of what? Contemplation of what one ought to be contemplating, namely the divine presence that inhabits all things. In India this contemplation is represented usually by the Buddha sitting, contemplating, bringing the *kuṇḍalinī* up, and so forth. This is the way of the monk who leaves the world, and turns inward, and contemplates inwardly.

But there is another way of contemplating and this is the way of the landscape art, and the Chinese art, and the way of Tao; namely, seeing the thing through all things. This is known as walking contemplation, you walk around. When Buddhism went from India to China, it was gradually assimilated to the Chinese attitude toward life, and in the eighth century this turn was given, *dhyāna,* or *ch'an,* meant rather walking than sitting. One was to undertake contemplation while walking, while being in the midst of life.

Then this Zen, or contemplative Buddhism, moved into Japan during the tenth, eleventh, and twelfth centuries. These are the high centuries of the Japanese medieval period, the so-called Heian period that Lady Murasaki portrayed in *The Tale of Genji.* Since Zen had to do with living life and experiencing life with alertness, it was a quite proper attitude for the knightly man.

Just so in the European High Middle Ages of the same time, you have the warrior-priest and the monk-knight. You have the Christian cross, which is, at the same time, held upside down, the sword. Likewise, in Japan you have the monastic discipline of the knightly monk, the samurai. I spoke of the fencing and sumo; these embody these principles of walking contemplation in athletics and in combat. So Zen Buddhism in Japan became associated with this way of the knights, which is a very military way. You find in Zen an emphasis on strict discipline.

In the course of the centuries, there has been a great development of Buddhism in Japan in many directions. But by curious irony the stress on seated meditation today in Japan is maintained most strongly in the Zen monasteries. It is simply amazing to walk into a Zen meditation hall where these young monks are seated with the rigidity of statues. Walking up and down is a man with a stick over a yard long over his shoulder as though it were a weapon, and any young meditator who looks as though sleep were overtaking him gets that stick right on the shoulder with a terrific wallop. This is Zen in Japan today. It is a technique of meditation and realization that is extremely strict.

In the tradition of Zen Buddhism in Japan and *ch'an* in China, we have two quite distinct types; one, that of meditating, and the other, that of walking. But please remember that when one walks in the Orient, one walks according to the rules of the society; it is freedom within the context of the society.

Looking at the practice of Zen in Japan today, you find nothing like the Zen beatniks, the wild *dharma* bums.[44] The attitude is rather one of strict life forms, and the realization—the *dhyāna,* the *zen,* the meditation, the contemplation—comes in the context of the highly formalized social situation.

Zen is the great source of the tea ceremony, and I think that when one thinks of Zen, it should be rather in the way of the excessive discipline of the game of the tea ceremony than in the way of the let-it-all-go-just-seek-nature, romantic way.

My personal feeling is that the Oriental lesson of art and life as a difficult game that we love to play is lost if Zen isn't understood in quite the way that we have been examining it. Without that context, there is no way for a Westerner truly to understand Eastern religion.

CHAPTER III

Vessels to the Farther Shore

Jainism: The Path of Withdrawal[45]

An interesting thing about the *jīva* is that this reincarnating monad, this reincarnating principle, is in essence absolutely pure. It is like a pure bubble. It has no quality. It has no individuality. It has no character. It is simply an expression of *ātman-Brahman.* But it is contaminated by karmic matter, by the stuff of the world. The whole world in fact is nothing but a seething mass of these monads trapped in gross matter.

This is a strict dualism: matter does not equal spirit. This is the point of view of the Jains. There is the pure self and there is that self in play in the world. All action contaminates that self, even what we call pure action. There are said to be six colors that pour into the soul, into this monad, through action. The grossest, roughest activity stains the soul black. Next comes the color dark blue. Then comes the color of smoke, then comes the color of fire, then yellow colors, and then white. The soul itself, in its pure state, is, remember, translucent. It isn't even white.

The universe in the Jain tradition is regarded as a great being in human form, sometimes as a female being—the world mother—sometimes as a male—in the form of a standing yogi. The plane of life on which we live is

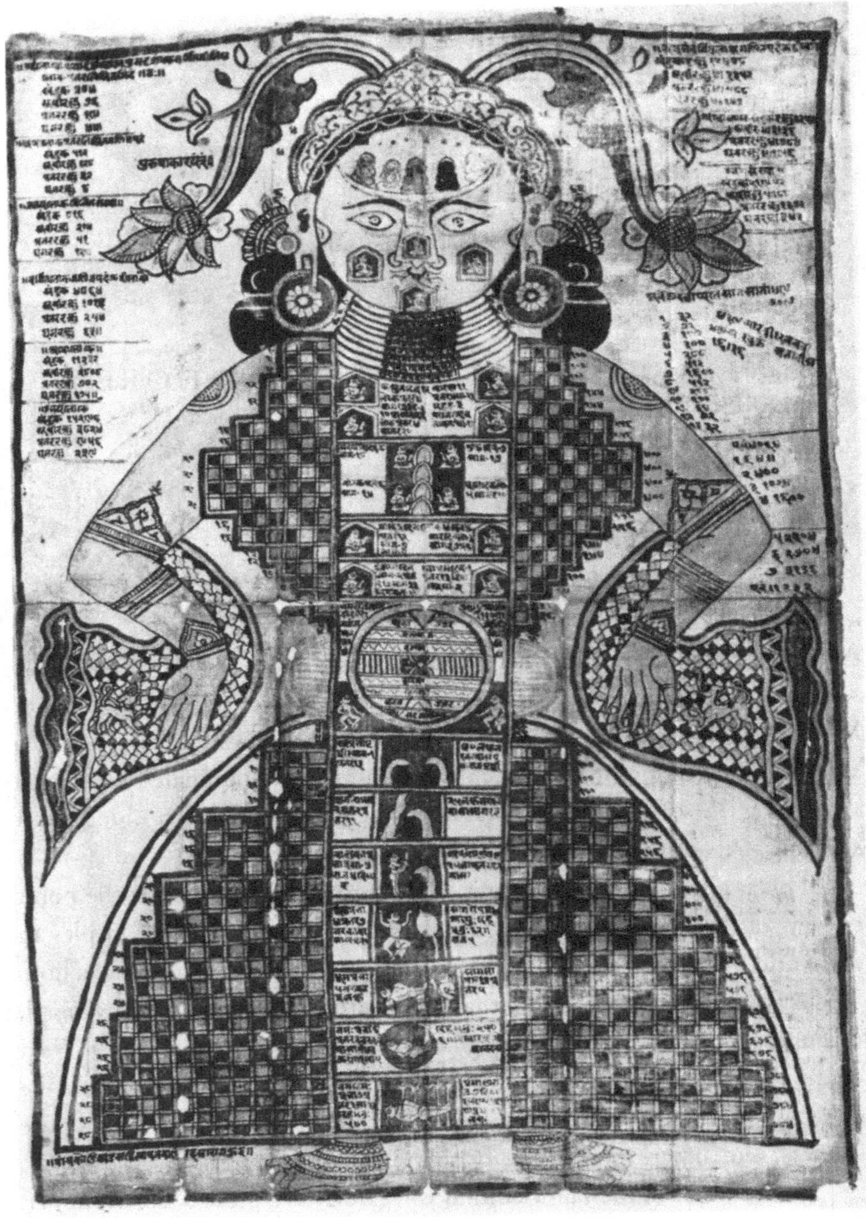

Figure 14. Jain world image in the form of a great goddess

right at the navel. The heavenly realms are up through the chest, and the infernal down to the toes. The beings in the lowest realms are of a dark, black color. Further up they are dark blue. Further up still, they are a smoky color, and just above that, fiery red. In the regions of the chest they are yellow. And at the top they are white. The goal of the yogi is to go up through these planes and end up finally at the very top of the cranium, the crown of the head. (This relates, in a way, to the seven stages of the *kuṇḍalinī* yoga, which probably is a late development of a tradition of this kind.) And at the top, the different victorious yogis—the conquerors, or *jinas*—are hanging, so to say, to the top of the head of the universe, like bubbles hanging from the ceiling. They have achieved *mokṣa,* "release," from the round of rebirth, *saṁsāra.* All individuality has been purged out, so that these illuminated ones are all exactly alike; you could not tell one from another. There is no such thing as personality or differentiation at this stage. And here again you get that distinctly Oriental motif of non-personality, the elimination of the ego as a goal in life. All personality is imperfection, is a sign of *karma,* a sign of commitment to some form of mistaken illusion.

The aim, over the course of many lifetimes, is to rise up among the *jinas* as a pure, unclouded bubble. To do this, you have to perform certain very strict yogic exercises.

This yoga of the Jains is based on the idea that you must stop acting, stop moving, stop eating, stop thinking, stop feeling, finally stop breathing. But it is no good dying unless you have quelled absolutely all interest in life. If there is one little part of "Oh, wouldn't it be nice?" left in you, you will be back.

Furthermore, as you proceed up the line, it is a fierce yoga. With each incarnation, you build up more pressure for coming back, so that in the last stages of this furious affair, the slightest little thing can dislodge you and you come right back down at the bottom.

"Life," as Schopenhauer said, "is something that should not have been."[46] If you take that seriously, well, out you go. Of course, it is not so easy to get out, because if you get out in resentment, you'll be back doing nasty things to people again. As we saw, the *jīva* must work its way free of this world back into union with *Brahman* without fear or desire. What you must do is quench your desire and fear; then you just go out like a light. You achieve *nirvāṇa;* you are blown out like a little flame: sputter, sputter, out.

Easily said. How do we get there?

There are two ways. One is through one's own strength. This is called in Japanese *jiriki,* "self power." The other is through what the Japanese call the Way of the Kitten: *tariki,* or "outside help." Just as a kitten requires its mother to pick it up by the scruff of the neck and carry it to safe ground, so some souls require the action of an outside agent to carry them beyond themselves.

Zen is the way of inside help; you do it yourself. In the great mythic world of the Bodhisattvas and the Buddhas, whose grace and mercy and compassion yield the energy that enables us to release ourselves from the bonds of illusion, on the other hand, you have the way of outside power. This is the way to myth. A mythic image is an outside power that comes to help you; through it you can achieve release from the bounds of the mundane world. We have various deities who represent the inferior powers of the lower *cakras,* but we also have ultimate deities that represent the ultimate power of ideation of the mind, and these are represented in the Buddha figures, in the Bodhisattva figures, and in Hinduism.

Emerging immediately after the time of the Upaniṣads, then, we have the traditions of withdrawal, of world negation: Theravāda Buddhism, Hinduism (both of which I will explore in greater detail later), and Jainism.

Jainism was extremely important and influential during the medieval period. It is now confined to a very small group—they lost numbers conspicuously in the twelfth, thirteenth, and fourteenth centuries—a small group now centered around Bombay, and up in Ahmedabad. In Jainism you have a very great stress on yoga. The Jain tradition includes a number of legends describing saviors or yogis who have appeared in the world from time to time, to the number of twenty-four. The latest one was a historical figure. His name was Mahāvīra. *Vīra* means "hero" (in the same sense as the Latin *vir,* which gives us "virtue") and *māha* means "great": the Great Hero. He was a contemporary of the Buddha, about 500 B.C., and his arguments against the Buddha are reported. But he had been preceded by twenty-three other Jain savior-teachers, the *tirthankaras.* The one before him, Pāśvanāta, had lived probably in the ninth century B.C., and before that another and another. The Jain dates, like all Indian dates, are simply wild. They carry us back before the Sun came into being. In any case, there is no doubt about it that this is an extremely ancient yogic tradition.

Mahāvīra was the last of the Jain *tirthankaras.* From his period and for the next centuries, the influence of the Jain tradition and the Upaniṣads seems to have become very important in India.

And the aim of this yoga—now here is a very important point—is death, literal death, but a death not before you have quenched in yourself *all desire for life.* If you kill yourself out of resentment, or out of discouragement, you'll be back. You must have quenched everything in you. So you follow a wonderful escalating schedule of vows, so that you limit what you do, stage by stage by stage, until finally you limit the number of steps you will take a day, the number of mouthfuls you will eat, until finally you go out like a light. It's extraordinary. This is the prime religion of *ahiṃsā,* of nonviolence—not to hurt any living thing because the whole world is a living thing.

The yogi in Jainism is really trying to die. The body is a mixture, according to this tradition, of spirit and matter, and all desire to live, all fear, etc., are a manifestation of matter, the physical aspect, of this combination. Whereas the repose, the eternal repose that is sought by the yogi, is entirely spiritual. By shutting the senses off, by sitting absolutely still, and by generating spiritual heat, one can burn out the matter from within oneself. But every time one acts, one attracts the contamination of more matter. So the tendency in Jainism—and this holds to this day—is gradually, during the course of many lives, to cut down activity. The layman begins by vowing never to kill or to injure any living flesh, and it is here that the idea of *ahiṁsā,* nonviolence, is extremely prominent and important. Nonviolence does not belong to the Aryans—it must come from the earlier, Dravidian tradition. The Aryans were quite violent, as we can see from the Homeric epics.

This is a paradox in India, the play of the violence of the *kṣatriya* warlords and the *ahiṁsā* of the others.

The next thing in connection with this tradition is a notion of reincarnation. So reincarnation belongs to the earlier tradition—that great round and progress of the soul that I have been talking about. And connected with this is the idea of *saṃsāra,* the never-ending wheel of the cycling ages. It is a round of sorrow: "All life is sorrowful," the Buddha's joyous lament, has roots in this tradition. And the only way to get out of it is by abstracting yourself through this extreme act of yoga.

The vows that are taken increase in severity and number as the individual's readiness improves from one incarnation to the next.

Now if you kill yourself to get out of this world, this will do no good, because you will be back: unburned-out *karma* will bring you back. The trick with Jainism is to eliminate gradually desires and fears, to eliminate them gradually by gradually increasing the number of negative vows that you take: the vows involve, toward the end, not moving—because when a person moves, he kills insects.

In Bombay, to this day, you will see the monks and nuns of the Jain sect wearing bands of gauze across the nose and mouth—they look like a doctor about to perform an operation. The reason is that one is not to breathe in insects and kill them, or to breathe in the air too strongly, because the air itself is alive. If you fall in the water, you are not to swim, because you would hurt the molecules of the water. You are to let yourself be gradually floated in to shore—and there you are not to dry yourself, but let the Sun dry you. This is an extreme attitude, and a very prominent one in this tradition. Also you will see the monks with brooms, gently brushing insects out of their path. A Jain will not drink anything in the dark, lest there should be some insect in the water. He will not eat a freshly cut apple: he must let it die, lose its vitality.

Ironically, since these people, the Jains, could not engage in any violent task or trade, they became bankers and industrialists, and thereby one of the richest groups in India. In Bombay you have this curious situation of an extremely archaic, world-renouncing religion with an extremely prominent and world-affirming laity. The laity supports the monks, of course, so that there is a gradual movement of the spirit away from the world.

Now this dualism of spirit and matter stands in radical contrast to the later non-dualism of Hinduism and Buddhism. And it is apparent that some kind of crisis took place during the upanishadic period. It apparently was the Aryan *brahmins* who, with their world-affirmative attitude, made the connection between these two, world and spirit, as two aspects of the same thing. So that the negativism of yoga gets dissipated in the Brahmanical tradition that I was describing, where all is *Brahman,* all is spirit. The world is a ripple or inflection of that great spirit. It is not absolutely different from and antagonistic to it, but is itself that very *Brahman.*

These two strains are very strong in India to this day: the negative and affirmative views. With philosophies that are very close, it is a little difficult sometimes to see what these differences are; nevertheless, they are there.

And now, there is one more thing that I'd like to discuss before I move to the next subject. In the course of the reincarnation in Jainism, the souls inhabit heavens and hells—the upper and lower levels of the cosmic body. The gods are those souls inhabiting the heavens, and the demons inhabit the hells. This means that there is no divine being superior to man. Man, in his higher stages, is a god. This is finally what one might call an atheistic religion. There is no Supreme Being, no creator of the world; the world has always been in rotation. The world itself, the cosmos itself, is regarded as a great being—you might call that God, if you wished. But it is not a being with a personality that enters into play.

So we have an atheistic religion, and the ultimate principle is that which inhabits man himself. This is the supreme thing. And this idea has made its way into all of Indian—and Oriental—thought. The Homeric Greeks offered to the gods, and the gods were super-beings. The Aryans in India also commenced by offering to the gods. But in the later stages, those Aryan gods are reinterpreted just as the Jain gods are. And so it is that previously I could tell you the story of Indra, the god in incarnation. There is no god but the universe itself—and man in the higher stages of spirituality. The yogi's aim is to go past the sphere of the gods.

There are two kinds of monks here. The strict monks are called "those clothed in space," *digambāra;* that is to say, the absolutely naked monks. They take off all their clothes, they pull off all their hair, they reject everything having to do with a reference to society, and you can see the images of these great stark-naked figures standing perfectly still in the posture known as *kayotsarga,* "dismissing the body"—let it go.

The other variety of monk is much less strict. This is known as *śvetambāra*—"dressed in white." They wear white garments. You can see them in the cities with these white garments, mouths protected. In Bombay one can see members of this order carrying out a ritual that—while it may seem a bit strange and even amusing—gets at the heart of the Jain philosophy. One day, I watched two chaps come along through the streets of Bombay with a cot full of bedbugs. As they walked, they called out, "Who will feed the bugs, who will feed the bugs?" Then some lady in the window would toss out a coin—she will feed the bugs. So one of the chaps lies down on the bed and the bugs have their dinner. Now both the monks and the lady are given karmic credit for assisting this inferior type of life, letting the bugs have this little enjoyment and move on through however many hundreds of incarnations, perhaps, to a *śvetambāra* monk saying, "Who will feed the bugs?"

The notion is that there are two principles—the soul and matter—and they are linked but distinct. And what you are trying to do is disassociate yourself entirely from the gross substance, clean yourself of karmic matter and become a perfect bubble and float, rising to the top of the universe as a bubble disassociated from the world, and there remain for all eternity beyond this round.

Now in contrast to that, there is the Buddhist doctrine, which is rather psychological than physiological. What the Buddha tells us needs to die is the zeal for life, is the *māyā* commitment. Ignorance is what leads to desire. Desire leads to action. Action leads to deeper ignorance. Ignorance leads to desire. Desire leads to action. How do you get out of this? Well, you can attack it either in the way of attacking desire, or action, or ignorance. The principal Buddhist way is to attack the ignorance. But you can also become inactive or control your action, or you can also regulate your desire.

Now the Buddha, too, would not have you act in the world at first. His doctrine was first interpreted as a monastic doctrine, as a doctrine of quitting the world just as the Jains quit the world, and the first communities of Buddhists did quit the world. But we find in Buddhism a very strong movement of living in the world without desire or fear but simply, as it were, in action. The fundamental notion is that once you have abandoned the world of desire and the world of fear, you undergo a psychological shift: your ego is dropped and you act simply as the world acts, in what is called spontaneity. You become, as it were, a tree. You become a plant. You live right out of yourself.

One can hear this thought in the words of Christ: "Consider the lilies of the field, how they grow; they toil not, neither do they spin: And yet I say unto you, that even Solomon in all his glory was not arrayed like one of these."[47] They are not anxious, they simply *are,* in all their glory. This idea swept the whole Orient, and it matched notions that were already present in China and Japan. In China we find this idea in the Taoist concept of *wuwei,* non-effort, action without striving, letting your life just roll. This idea is the basic Buddha idea, and it broke the grip of this literal yoga of killing yourself. And when you have detached yourself like this, you are like burnt string. Śaṅkara, the great Hindu teacher of the eighth century A.D., taught that when a person has purged himself of ego, he is like a string that has been burnt lying on the ground; it looks like a string still, but if you blow on it, it wisps away—it isn't there. And so it is with a person who has quenched his commitment to ego and has pulled back. He is, as it were, in the center, and life moves through him in a rolling process. This is the basic ideal, I would say, for the individual living in the world, whether in Buddhism, in Taoism, or in Hinduism.

Hinduism: The Pursuit and Escape of Dharma[48]

Impersonal Divinity

The first thing one must realize is that Hinduism is an ethnic religion: that is to say, one is born a Hindu. One can make a very valid analogy that Hinduism is related to Buddhism about as Judaism is to Christianity, not in terms of historical development but in terms of membership, as it were. Where Christianity was originally a reform movement of Judaism, both Buddhism and Hinduism developed during the upanishadic period out of the Aryan Vedic tradition. Hinduism was originally a restoration of the old Vedic tradition, with the addition of Dravidian yoga.

Now, just as one is born a Jew, one is born a Hindu. Not only is one born a Hindu, one is born in a certain social stratum of the Indian tradition: a *brahmin,* a *kṣatriya,* a *vaiśya,* or a *śūdra.* One professes Buddhism; one confesses Christianity. Hinduism and Judaism are what I shall call ethnic religions; they are religions of a very ancient lineage—both practices date back not quite three thousand years, and the current practitioners are, for the most part, descendants of the founders.

Buddhism, Christianity, and Islam, on the other hand, are creedal faiths; it is what you believe, not whom you are descended from that matters. These are world religions because anybody can profess them. Anybody can't be a Jew, anybody can't be a Hindu—you have to be born thus. One can convert, but it is not something Jewish or Hindu practice encourages. Anybody, however, can become a Christian, a Buddhist, a

Muhammadan. These three religions, therefore, have been dispersed into areas of truly varied culture forms. Buddhism, for instance, appears in Tibet, in China, in Korea, in Japan, but also in Ceylon, in Burma, in Thailand, Vietnam—and it used to be also in Sumatra and Java. You know the spread of Christianity on both sides of the world. Islam, too, can be found from the gates of Europe to Indonesia. And all three have found adherents in the New World. Creedal religions are typically initiated by a single prophet, a single teacher who extracts the spiritual quintessence, as it were, of the ethnic religion from which he derives. The life of the teacher becomes, then, a symbol of the doctrines.

In an ethnic religion like Hinduism, there is very great stress placed upon ritual law. There is often little distinction made between ritual virtue *(bhakti)* and what we, having inherited our notions from the Greeks, would call ethics. For instance, one reads in the Old Testament of a man who is found picking up sticks on Saturday, on the Sabbath. Moses asks, "God, what should be done about this man?"

The answer comes back, "He should be stoned to death. He was breaking a ritual law."

Similarly, in Hinduism most of the laws and doctrines that we will look at are ritual laws of this kind. They have nothing to do with a general concept of human ethics. We have been translating *dharma* as "virtue," but in truth the Hindu laws do not encourage "virtue" in the sense of an abstract psychological, ethical ideal. These are laws that are made specifically to keep a certain group of people together and to differentiate them from other people.

In Judaism, you have the Jewish community set apart as a priestly race, the holy race. Aside from a basic ritualization of everyday life, that's the real function of the kosher laws—you can't eat your food in anyone else's house, the people must be together. Similarly in Hinduism, the castes are divided from each other and are set off from the non-Hindus as well. These two religions come from almost exactly the same period of time.

In Hinduism there are special rules for each caste, because here you have not simply one sort of religious group, you have a whole social structure. You have the priests, you have the governing caste, you have the merchant caste, and you have the servant caste. In India, to this day, people are separated from each other to such an extent that everybody is untouchable to everybody else. I remember the amazement of my life when I met a splendid young *brahmin* youth when I was a young man myself; he was over here and preaching and teaching—I won't tell you who he was, though you would know his name.[49] He was the son of a *brahmin* family, and he told me that when he went back to India, he could not eat with his father because he had crossed the water. He had left India and had eaten with lechers; if he were Jewish, the father would have used the word *goyim,* "gentiles." These are the people who are not of the holy society. The young man had shared the table with unclean people, and therefore he couldn't eat with his father.

This is a very important point to remember about the great old traditional religions out of which these later creedal religions have developed. The current situation—the relationship of traditional Hindu culture to the secular cosmopolitan society—is extremely complicated, and one can only feel anxiety for the problem of the Indian psyche.

In traditional Hinduism, each caste has its own laws, its own morality, its own place in the society, and the individual is given so many laws to attend to that his whole life is spent doing what he *ought* do and he never has a moment to think, What would I like to do? The function of these laws is to bind the individual to the group absolutely so that he is not what we would call an individual. In Sanskrit there is no word that means individual. In traditional Indian art, individuals are not represented; rather, what are represented are typical *brahmins,* typical princes, typical merchants. Only the gods in their avatars are represented in a recognizable way: Viṣṇu's avatars—Kṛṣṇa and so on—with their blue skin. Everything about the individual that you meet on the street proclaims his caste: the dress that he wears; the name that he bears; even his physical character. Since people have married only within the caste for thousands of years, these groups have essentially become separate races. If you travel in India and have the good fortune to get outside of the Cook's Tours area and meet people of different social orders or see them, you'll know within days how to distinguish the people walking down the street: you can tell when you see them, That's a *brahmin,* that's a merchant, this one is a *śūdra.* And it is not merely a matter of bearing and material possession that signals these differences, as they would in the West. Remember, there are wealthy, proud *śūdras* and humble, poor *brahmins:* everything about the person proclaims his identification with the caste.

The goal of all this is to make the individual forget that he's an individual, to make him lose the sense of himself as a freely willing, freely judging, unique being. The highest caste is called the *brahmins;* in Sanskrit, that is *brāhmaṇa*. Now that long *ā* with the line, or macron, over it at the beginning means "related to." So *brāhmaṇa* means "having to do with *Brahman*," that divine power which we have been examining—the source and being of the universe.

The *brahmins* are those who know how to direct that energy into the channels of the society at large so that it animates and fosters and forwards the aims of the social group. They do this by means of their rites, which consist primarily of two aspects: one is the act to perform; and the other is the hymn, or the voice, or the word that is pronounced in relation to the action. These hymns, these words, these magical-power syllables come from that body of literature known as the Vedas. That word *veda* comes from a Sanskrit root *vid*, which means "to know"; *veda* means "knowledge." These Vedas represent the knowledge of the divine order of the universe as revealed in the books in which these hymns and their musical intonations appear. Just like the Hebrew scriptures, these books are considered to be a direct revelation of the divine law; the Sanskrit word is *śruti*, which means "what is heard." These hymns were not invented, according to doctrine; these hymns were first heard by the ancient seers, the ancient *hearers* if you will. Where this revealed law differs from the Pentateuch is that they come as manifestations not of the revelation of a divine being but of the revelation of the order of the universe itself.

As I have already said, the divine beings in the Orient are personifications of the power of the universe, but the universe is there from beginning to end, and there was no beginning and there will be no end. It was not created; rather, it is in being, it is in process. The perfectly impersonal, mechanical laws of this process reveal themselves through the Vedas. The truth revealed in the Vedas includes not only the words that are sung to evoke the powers, but also the actions. These ritual actions—every movement, every intonation—are a precious legacy that has come down from the days of the Vedic Aryans. They are communicated exactly from one generation to the next, so that it has come down as an unmodified heritage. The teacher's function is not to criticize, not to judge, not to interpret, but to render without modification what he received from his teacher, and so forth, and so forth, and so forth. The teacher is therefore to become, as it were, a completely transparent glass; he isn't there. This not being there is the ultimate aim of Indian spirituality; the *brahmins* are, due to their duty to lose themselves in the rites, the topmost caste.

There was a very interesting moment in Indian religious development that occurred around 800 B.C. when the implications of the Vedas began to be discussed in theological discourse. This, as we have discussed, is the moment of the birth of the Upaniṣads. Here is the realization that sparked this transformation: since through our rites we can control the gods, our rites are stronger than the gods. Since the *brahmins* know how to manipulate these rites, the *brahmins* are stronger than the gods; the *brahmins* are the strongest beings in the universe. This remains the Indian concept to this day; that is to say, the traditional Indian complex still operates under this assumption. If you don't believe that traditional India is still operative, think of the riots that have broken out around the anti–cow slaughter campaigns. There is a ground base of traditionalism and conservatism and antiquity there that is absolutely immeasurable.

The second caste is called the *kṣatriya.* This comes from a Sanskrit root *kṣat,* meaning "to protect, to defend," just like the police department. The *kṣatriya* are the governing cast, the kings and princes. The word has been translated frequently as "warrior caste," but we would not call Queen Elizabeth a member of the warrior caste; these are the aristocrats, the nobility. Their function is to govern the people—and here's a very important point—in terms of the law revealed by the *brahmins.* Again one can make a comparison with the Bible or with the Hebrew tradition; the laws of Leviticus and Deuteronomy and so forth are not regarded as invented by man: they are revealed of God. Similarly, in India the laws by which the *kṣatriya,* or aristocrats, govern are regarded as revealed; man has no choice in this matter. One cannot appeal to the next meeting of the legislature to adopt an amendment or appeal a law that one does not like. These laws are as immutable as the laws of physics.

It's from the Greeks that we get the idea that the human intelligence is competent to determine prudent, noble, appropriate aims for human life and to contrive laws by which those aims may be achieved. This is not the traditional view, either in the Bible or in the Hindu tradition. The traditional view is that the law comes from the universe—or from the creator of the universe in the biblical tradition—and is imposed upon man. It is man's function to adjust himself to that law, to live by it, not to criticize it. One does not ask, "But this is insane, why should a human being do this?" Do it, kill the man who picked up sticks on Saturday.

This is the way the traditional laws operate in India, so that the function of the *kṣatriya* is to administer the laws that the *brahmin* knows through his study of the revelation; administer them to see that they are obeyed. The revelation, the *brahmin* who knows it, the prince who administers it and sees to it that the law is obeyed—all are expressions of pure *dharma,* duty. There is no discrimination here, no volition. The notion of law as a convention, as a social contract, does not exist.

When I drive in my car and the red light comes on—well, I stop; then, when the green light goes on, I get going again. If I were to cross against the red light, I would have my eyes open for a policeman (and other cars)—not for God almighty. I would not be offending the laws either of God or of the universe but of the local conventions. This is our idea of law; you violate humanity or the local convention, but not the universe. This is a quite different psychology from that circumscribed in the Vedas and the Pentateuch, and we must bear this in mind when we're thinking of the traditional mind.

The third caste is known as the *vaiśya.* Their name comes from a root *viś,* which means "to settle." This is the third estate, the caste of money, the caste of property ownership—what we would call the substantial body of the community. These people are the merchants, the landowners, the bankers, and so forth. Their function is to raise their family in decency and prosperity, to make money. The *brahmin* lives for what he conceives to be truth, namely the truth of the Vedas. The *kṣatriya* lives for justice and impersonally administered authority. The merchant lives for prosperity and the abundance of life. He pays his taxes and pays his tithes and so supports the princes and the priests.

These three castes are called the "twice-born," or the "*āryan*" castes. *Āryan* is a Sanskrit word meaning "noble." These are the castes for whom the Hindu tradition is designed.

Separate from them, quite apart—a different race, different species, different character altogether—are the so-called *śūdra;* this comes from a root that means "to suffer." These are the artisans, the peasants, the workers, and what we would call the outcasts. They are not assimilated into the Aryan tradition. They are regarded as totally other. They are of two orders: one, those from whom a *brahmin* may accept water; the other, those from whom a *brahmin* may not accept water. Why may the *brahmin* not accept water from these lower *śūdras?* Because he would become contaminated. These people, the *śūdras,* are regarded not only as socially but also as spiritually low. It is as though they were diseased and to touch the unclean *śūdra,* that is to say those from whom one cannot take water, is to contaminate yourself with a spiritual infection. The ruthless avoidance of these people, what is, from our standpoint, the horror of their lives, is a function of the belief that they are infectious, like lepers; they are spiritual plague bearers.

I have discussed the Indian law books, the so-called Laws of Manu. *Manu* is a word related to our word *man,* also *mentality. Manu* is the sort of primordial man image of India. The Laws of Manu say in one passage that I remember reading with amazement, that if a *śūdra* hears the recitation of the Vedas, even by accident, he shall have boiling lead poured into his ears.

The Vedas are power, in both senses of the word; they are like atomic secrets. They are the powers by which the *brahmins* direct the energies of the universe, and this power must not be leaked to the subject people.

Before the English rule, an unclean *śūdra* dying of thirst as he came into a village compound where the twice-born lived—he couldn't touch the water there. Nobody could give it to him either, because how could you get it to him?

Say he wasn't dying, that he was simply passing through the village. He would have to wear a spittoon so that his saliva wouldn't fall on the Earth and contaminate it. This is fierce.

Dharma and Sat

This seems inequitable to us, to say the least; not so to the Indian. Why not? Remember that fundamental to all Oriental social thinking is the concept of reincarnation. Central to this concept is the notion that through many, many lives we go through a sort of school—the school of the universe, the school of the world, the school of rebirths. I think of these four castes—*śūdra, vaiśya, kṣatriya,* and *brahmin*—as the freshman, sophomore, junior, and senior classes, at the top of the school system. Below that we have people who have had the misfortune not even to be born in India, like ourselves—we're in high school still. Further down we find the animals—although the animals born in India are more fortunate than ourselves. Below that is the vegetable world and the elemental physical world. The objects around you—the paper on this page, the water that you are perhaps drinking, the pebbles in the soles of your shoes—are souls on the way up. Think of a pop bottle: when you take the top off, the bubbles come up. Where do they come from? Where do they go? Who knows—the void—but there they are coming up just the same. Just so the souls bubble up, from mineral form through the vegetables, and so on, and so on, and so on, and so on, and so on, and so on . . . The whole world is an educational institution and every creature in it is trying to learn a lesson.

What is the lesson that is to be learned? The lesson to be learned is egolessness, to cancel the noise "I." As they say in Sanskrit, *ahaṃkārā,* "making the noise I." Now, as I pointed out, in the Orient there is no distinction made between "I"—what we call the ego—and "I want"—what we call the id. So "I" is "I and mine." This is my body, these are my thoughts, these are my words: the lesson of the school is to get rid of that, not to be there. So you can see now, the kicking around that the *śūdra* gets is his lesson. He is losing the sense of "I"; he is learning how to live in accord with the law of the universe in terms of his range of understanding.

Now between our college years there come the holidays, those lovely times of summer, and, if the student has lived a good year, that student will go on a holiday somewhere. Similarly, if a person has lived a good life—has learned the lesson of that life—he will go on a holiday somewhere. Where? To one of the heavens—a heaven in accord with his capacity. If his desire is sensual, if he lives for *kāma,* or sexual delight, he will go to a heaven of that kind, a celestial seraglio. If his desire is the contemplation of high thoughts, he will go to a heaven of that kind. If his potentiality is to go beyond thought, he will go to a heaven of that kind.

If he has lived a bad year, however, he will go to a summer school, and once he is there, really tough, thuggish professors will be banging it into him with clubs—that's hell. Now the heavens and hells are inhabited by human beings between lives, and these human beings are what men call gods and demons. That is to say, there is no ontological, essential difference whatsoever between gods and men.

Gods are simply men and women between lives, in the heavens enjoying the fruits of a good life lived. Then, when the reward bank is used up, back you come for another life. It is in human life that the fulfillment is to be achieved, not in heaven.

Now just as the ultimate goal of college is to graduate, the goal of life is to get out of this school, never to come back, to be absolutely nobody at all, to have learned the lesson perfectly, to have erased yourself. This is a hard thing for us in the West to comprehend. The personality, the individuality, that intelligible character, that thing that is you in our view endures; that is the final term, to find yourself as a self different from other selves. When Dante and Aeneas and Odysseus descend into the underworld, they recognize the people there. The individual personalities persist, even after the individual has shuffled off this mortal coil.

If you were to go to a Hindu heaven or hell, or a Buddhist heaven or hell, or a Jain heaven or hell, you would see lots of people there, but you couldn't recognize any of them, nor could they recognize you—not even the souls of your parents or your spouse. They wouldn't remember their earlier lives, the lives that got them there. They are gods, living as gods, thinking of themselves as gods, just as we are human beings, living as human beings, thinking of ourselves as human beings; whereas only a few years ago we too were gods in a heaven, the heaven between the last life and this one. We simply don't remember that. And when you get to the heaven next time, you won't remember this life at all. You won't know why you are there. You will simply think, Oh, I'm a god. The development here is absolutely impersonal. You are playing a role. There is no individual whatsoever: the main point of the whole curriculum is to get the student to understand that idea.

Now, if you are obeying the rules, obeying the rules, obeying the rules, you don't have the opportunity to develop as an individual. This is a point that I think is terribly important. Let us just think of this psychologically for a moment. What is the function of the ego, of "I"? There are two aspects. The first is "I want," the simple childlike ego. This is countered in the nursery by "thou shalt." The child wants but mommy and daddy know better: thou shalt. Once it is internalized, this "thou shalt" is called, in

Freudian psychology, the superego. In a traditional culture, the goal is to go from "I want" straight to "thou shalt," to incarnate the laws that are the local "thou shalt" system.

That's not our ideal. Our ideal is that the little growing individual should develop his own judgment, that he should become a self-responsible, judging individual. He should control his own "I want" through his own matured judgments as to what is proper for himself, for his friends, for his country, for his world.

In Freudian terms, the ego is split and the "I want," the id, is subjugated to the moderation of the ego. That is to say, we ask the individual to develop a creative, critical, self-responsible personality. "Billy, do you want ice cream or cake, do you want chocolate or vanilla? Make up your mind. Johnny, do you want to marry Susan or Betty? Make up your mind." Not so in the Orient; you get chocolate ice cream—whether you like it or not—and you marry Betty—and you never saw her before. There is absolutely no development of the critical personality. The ideal is that there is nobody there but that the tradition is coming through, coming through, coming through without alteration.

Now this process of living your duty goes by a name we will recognize: *dharma.* This is the key word of Hinduism. It is from a Sanskrit root *dhṛ,* which means "to support." You perform your duty and so support the universe. The universe is alive. The Sun performs its duty, the Moon performs its duty, the mice perform their duty, the cats perform theirs, the *brahmins* perform theirs, the *śūdras* perform theirs, and by this—everyone performing his duty—the universe is held in form. By following your *dharma,* you hold the universe in form.

The word for truth is *satya*—perhaps you remember Gandhi's *satyagrāha. Grāha* means "gripping," so together the phrase means "holding to truth." That word *satya* comes from a Sanskrit root *sat,* which means "to be." A person who performs his duty *is* something. *Sat:* he is.

The feminine form of *sat* is *satī.* We know this word from its anglicized form, suttee—the act of the wife who burns herself to death on her husband's funeral pyre. The wife who burns herself to death on her husband's funeral pyre *is* a wife. The Indians don't say that such a wife "commits suttee"; the Indians say that she "becomes *satī*"—she becomes something. The person who does not perform his duty is *a-sat,* nothing. You achieve your character by doing as your *dharma* demands, not by deciding what you want to do or what you think would be proper to do. I think it can be said that all of Indian life is an act of suttee.

I have two little stories to tell to give a sense of this. The Indian anecdotes are very vivid, memorable, and they illustrate the point in a very strong way.

This first story has to do with *sat,* with performing your duty; it comes from the second century B.C., from a Buddhist work called the Milindapañha. It is thought in a sort of popular way that a person who has performed his duty perfectly throughout his life can perform magic simply by saying, If I have done so-and-so all my life without fail, really, truly, then let such and such take place, and it will take place. This is called an Act of Truth.

This story takes place during the third century B.C., during the reign of the great Buddhist emperor Aśoka. One year, the monsoons were particularly heavy, and the Ganges was rising and threatening to flood the capital city of Pataliputra, which is now called Patna. The emperor went down to the bank of the river to watch this; all the people were there, calling to him, "The river's coming up, what's going to happen?"

As it approached the level of great danger, Aśoka called out, "Is there nobody here who can perform an Act of Truth and cause the waters of the Ganges to flow back upstream?"

The *brahmins,* the priests, consulted themselves, but none of them could perform an Act of Truth. They were *brahmins* because they had lived lives perfectly in earlier incarnations, but in this one not one of them was perfect.

The *kṣatriyas* could do no better—not even the emperor himself—nor could the *vaiśyas.*

Way down the line was an old prostitute. Her name was Bindumatī, and she began muttering around, saying, "I have an Act of Truth."

"Well!" her neighbor said, "Bindi, get going, for heaven's sake!"

So Bindumatī draws herself inward and in her own soul pronounces the Act of Truth, and of course, what do you know, the river does indeed begin to flow back upstream.

Understandably, everybody is enormously excited. Aśoka asks who performed the Act of Truth, and the word comes rippling up to the emperor that it was none other than his lowliest subject, Bindumatī. He stands for a moment in amazement, because it is a funny thing about doctrines of religion: one knows what they are, but one never thinks they really work. Then the emperor goes down the way and there is Bindumatī. He calls her a string of names: "You despicable, loathsome old whore, you mean to say you have an Act of Truth?"

Quite calmly and humbly she responds, "I have an Act of Truth that would turn the world of the gods upside down if I wanted it to."

Somewhat intimidated, the emperor says, "What is your Act of Truth?"

Bindumatī, the *śūdra,* says, "It is as follows: if in the performance of my duty, I have not fawned on the wealthy, the handsome, or those of high caste, nor despised the poor, the lowly, and the ugly, but have always given due service for the money. Let the waters flow back upstream." And so the river had flowed at her command since she was pure *dharma. Satī:* she was. There was nobody there. She was gold; she had no judgment, she was doing her duty. That's the way India is supposed to work.

Once she had done her duty, did the emperor say, "Bindumatī, you've saved the city! Come, we'll put a monument up. Sit on the throne, you're queen for the day"? Nothing of the kind, not in that lifetime. Next lifetime perhaps she would be queen of Benares, but not then. She was a *śūdra;* that is her function—mice cannot become lionesses. This is something to remember with respect to the caste system. By performing his duty no matter where, the individual participates in the glory and power of the universe and becomes a conduit of that power. Nobody *chooses* to do anything; everybody is doing what he ought, and so this grand thing, the universe, spins on.

One goes to India and one sees the horror of it, and by god it is appalling what one sees; the words for poverty and squalor that we use don't touch what we see there. Yet when you are there and the shock has finally been absorbed, there comes this realization of peace, of radiance.

Lewis Mumford once said, "Values emerge from life on all its levels."[50] But they won't emerge if you're criticizing it; they will emerge only if you go with it. This is the traditional point of view. You come in on this level, live it, perform the duty—I'm speaking now of Indian terms. Don't say, "Oh gee, I ought to be up there, I ought to be down here, somebody's cheating me, this guy's getting more than I am"—live it. Judge your life not in terms of what the other fellow's getting but in terms of whether you're really doing it. This is the glory of India, it's the thing that made it great once, it's the thing that's supporting it in its horror now. So much then for the idea of *sat,* being something: you are something insofar as you're a social being by doing your job; and they do it, they do it well.

There is another story, to illustrate the relationship of ego to *dharma.* This one is a more gentle story, and it concerns a member of that worthy profession, the teacher. In India the word "teacher" is *guru;* however, this means something very different from what teacher means for us. "Teacher" for us—nowadays at any rate—means somebody who communicates information to you and gives you certain guidance in your life and helps you through the crises that may crop up. Guru means a person who himself is your model; the student is meant to identify with the teacher, to become as the teacher; the teacher became as his teacher, and so there is nobody there. The teacher simply transmits the ideal, the *dharma,* down the line.

Now this story concerns a student who arrived one day late. The teacher says, "You're late. Where have you been, what's the matter here?"

"Well," the student says, "I could not get here. I live on the other side of the river. The river was in flood, there was no ferry, the fording place was too deep, and so I could not get here."

"Well," says the teacher, "you are here now. Did the ferry come? Did the river come down?"

The student shakes his head. "No, nothing changed on the river."

"Well, how did you get here?"

The student says, "I thought of my teacher. I thought, My teacher is the vehicle of truth to me, he is my god, he is my oracle, I will think about my teacher and I'll walk across the water, and so I did. I thought, *Guru, guru, guru,* and I walked across the flood. Here I am."

Wow, thought the teacher, I didn't know I could do that. Of course, the teacher hadn't done it.

When the student goes, the teacher thinks this was in him. He says, "I'll go to try this thing. I've got to see how this works." So he looks around to see if anybody's watching. When he is sure he is alone, he goes down to the water and looks at the rushing torrent. He thinks, I'm going to do it. He thinks, *I, I, I.* He steps out onto the river... and he sinks like a stone.

The only reason one can walk across water is that there is nobody there; one is pure spirit, *spiritus,* wind. In Sanskrit, this is *prāṇa.* That teacher in the student's mind was a communicator of truth. In his own mind, he was an "I," and an "I" has weight and sinks.

So the first thing to understand about Hinduism and the individual is caste and the idea of *dharma,* of living one's duty.

The Stages of Life

Now we come to one more important theme, the *aśramas*—that means "disciplines." These are the disciplines proper to the different stages of life. According to the Hindu model, life is divided in the middle—this is a wonderful concept but isn't one that I recommend. Life is divided in the middle when the first gray hairs arrive. The first half of life, in the traditional view, is to be lived in the village, in the society, performing one's social *dharma.* The second half of life is to be lived in the forest, performing yoga to achieve absolute illumination.

This is the way in which India has synthesized the two diametrically opposed orders of social commitment on the one hand and, on the other, social dissociation in order to achieve inwardness and absolute transcendence. For India social life and all this that I have been talking about is simply a preparation; you are diminishing the force of ego. In the forest you must erase it absolutely, or you must try.

Each half of life is itself divided into two parts. The first part of each half is to be spent learning, and the second part in realization. The first quarter of life, therefore—the first fifteen years or so—is spent as a student. This time is called *brahmacarya,* which means "going in Brahman."

The second quarter of life is *gṛhastha,* the period of the householder. One is married—even though one never saw the wife or husband before. The family and family marriage brokers have provided a perfectly proper person according to your caste. You can read in Indian newspapers today columns advertising for wives. All this is done by the family and brokers—the little boy or girl knows nothing about it. The crisis comes at the end of the ceremony when the veil between bride and groom is removed and each sees the other, and that's it—*sat, satī.* This other young person is your *dharma* from here on out. This is a crisis indeed, particularly for the wife, who will probably be expected to throw herself on this whatever-it-is's funeral pyre some fine day.

The couple set up house. They see to following their *dharma,* as it is defined by their caste and by their family obligations. The first duty of a householder is to beget children; this is the duty to the ancestors in honor and in gratitude for the life that one has received; one passes it on.

Then, once the couple are in their early thirties—if they started seeing to their duty early enough—the father will have a son ready to take over the obligations of the *gṛhasthaya*—the householder. Now comes the time of the father's departure. Now, at midlife, the man is expected to go into the forest.

These households are great patriarchal households. There is a beautiful ritual where the father communicates his *dharma* to the oldest son—all of the rites, the marriage rites, the rites of the first night, and so forth, are beautiful. The individual is identified with cosmic forces and so forth and impersonal though it is, it achieves a kind of religious glory. The father communicates his *dharma* to his son and with the advice of his guru or his *brahmin,* goes into the forest.

Now we're in the first part of the second half of life, the third stage. This is called the period of entering the forest—*vānaprastha.* Now, one is not to enter the forest too early—one must have fulfilled one's *dharma,* one must be spiritually ready—indeed, a *śūdra* would have to wait until he went through another lifetime—or ten—and achieved the proper readiness of the soul. Just so, a Jew who wishes to explore the mystical aspects of his religion is supposed to wait until he is forty, married, and steeped in the study of scripture and law before undertaking to study the Cabala.

So our well-prepared fellow goes to a guru in the forest, who will teach him yoga, or at least will estimate his capacities and give him religious exercises appropriate to his spiritual development. Maybe the guru will just give him a copy of the Bhagavad Gītā, or the guru may say, "Dig a hole in the ground, put yourself in it, leave your nose out, and stay there for a couple of months." Depending on the readiness and the needs of the student, the training may run all the way from the mildest religious exercise to the most severe.

What is the goal of this yoga? Well, when Western people become sentimental about the Orient, they have lots of nice, warm thoughts about yoga, but the fierceness and ruthlessness of this might curl your hair. Up to this point, you lived your life performing your duties: no ego, no ego, no ego. But there were certain things you *did* like, certain things you *didn't* like, certain memories you cherish, certain memories that give you pain. In the ultimate yoga, you are to erase all those experiences so that you can't tell the difference between a pain and a pleasure, so that you can't tell the difference between a foul stench and a glorious perfume, so that you can't tell the difference, as they say, between gold and mud. You must kill even the energy of your cells to cling to life; you must shatter the life in yourself so that there is nothing there. That is the goal of this yoga. That is the purpose behind these fantastic austerities. In some of the Hindu systems, this is understood in an extremely physical way: that you really are killing the body in you, killing the will to life, killing the fear of death, killing everything in you.

In Buddhism, we will see that the aim is to kill the bonds of life psychologically: you are not really to kill yourself off but to become, as it were, burnt-out ash, like Śaṅkara's burnt string; it looks like a string, but blow and it isn't there. The illuminated man looks like a man but there is nobody there, there is absolute egolessness. When in your yoga you have achieved that realization, it is called release, *mokṣa.* Buddhists call this place of release *nirvāṇa*—where winds do not blow.

You remember the first verse of Genesis, when the wind of God broods over the waters, the wind that starts the ripple of the waters of life; stop that wind, and there is no creation, there is nothing. When that has been achieved within the individual, he is literally nobody. He now need not practice yoga because he has achieved the aim of yoga: he is a burnt string. But his body is still in momentum, it's still there; he becomes what is called a *sannyāsī,* a wandering monk or a wandering saint. India is full of these men—a lot are fakirs, but you find many of the real thing too. As with the Jainist monks, you find two types of these holy men: those who wear a garment that suggests a burial shroud and those that are absolutely naked. Since clothing in India indicates your caste and also indicates a social reference within the caste, nakedness indicates that you have gone beyond caste; you have achieved absolute indifference to the world.

Now, after you have finished your dinner, what do you do with the garbage? There were no refrigerators in the old days, and no garbage trucks, so you look at the door; there will be a yogi or two there, with their hands held out if they're naked or a bowl if they're wearing a shroud. You give them the garbage—that is all that they ask for. These men have lived their duty, they have done it, and now they are wandering, dead leaves.

Ask them questions, religious questions; some of them will not be speaking, but others will teach. Here's an important point: they teach not from theory but from experience. They have experienced the ultimate aim of Hindu religious life. Clergymen—and the *brahmins* in India are the clergy—teach from having read the right books. That is an altogether different thing. These *sannyāsī* teach from the source from which the books came. These wandering ascetics constitute in India an actual living refreshment of the archaic tradition. I have met them and talked to them; they are experiencing today the truth that was the source of the Vedas. The *sannyāsī's* connection to the original source of truth is experienced as valid, self-evident. Nobody can refute it. Nobody can tell me there is no such thing as an elephant if I have seen an elephant; just so, nobody can tell me there is no such thing as release if I have experienced release. These men know and they constitute a traditional, conservative, terrific power in India.

Buddhism: The Flower of the World[51]

The Life of the Buddha

Buddhism was the first of the world religions, as contrasted with the ethnic religions, the local religions into which one is born. One is born a Hindu; one is born a Jew; one chooses or professes Buddhism, Christianity, or Islam. These are the three world religions and, curiously, the dates of their founding are each spaced at intervals of about five hundred years. The Buddha's dates are 563 to 483 B.C. Jesus' dates are from perhaps 2 or 3 B.C. to something like A.D. 30, and Muhammad died A.D. 632.

The traditional or ethnic religions are long-growing, historical affairs, in which the doctrine of the religion is spelled out in the history of the society. Each of the world religions, however, stems from the illumination of a single teacher, and the essence of the doctrine is rendered in the legendary life of that teacher—Gautama, Jesus, Muhammad.

The life of the Buddha is the clue to the sense of his teaching, so I'll point out some of the major crises in the story of his life and extrapolate some of the basic tenets of Buddhism from there. Now, when we have the legend of a man like this, it doesn't matter whether it is true or false with respect to historical fact. It has nothing to do with fact. It has to do with the rendition and symbolic forms of the sense of the doctrine. This is as true of Christianity and Islam as it is of Buddhism. But Buddhism is more comfortable with this concept.

According to the legend, then, when the Buddha, then named Siddhārtha Gautama Śākyamuni, was born, he had a number of unusual markings—*cakras,* or wheels, on his hands and feet (as we have seen), a bump on the top of his head, and so on. His mother went by the very apropos name of Māya, and young Siddhārtha was born literally out of her side, and walking. His father, a petty king in Nepal, had the sages and astrologists predict something about this child based on these signs. They said, "He is destined to be either a world teacher or a world monarch."

The father, being himself a king and favoring the kingly profession, hoped that his son would not be a world teacher and set about to fix things so that he would be a world monarch. He did this by preventing him from seeing or experiencing anything the least bit unpleasant, so that he would never be disturbed to the extent of questioning life. Now, if you want to prepare a young man to have a real shock when he finds out what life is, this is the way to do it. The king turned his son over to a wonderful bevy of singing girls and maidens, and they took care of him so that he should never experience anything the least bit unpleasant.

Then, one fine day, when he is aged about eighteen, in that critical period of his life, the young prince says to his people, "I would like to go forth from the palace." So the father sees to it that there is no sight unpleasant within seeing distance. He clears the streets and sprinkles them with lotus petals and this kind of thing, and the young man drives forth with his charioteer. People are looking from the housetops and all—here is their prince for the first time, making an excursion into the city.

The deities see to it, however, that he has an experience; in the prince's path, they place a sick man. The young man asks, "What's this?" His charioteer says, "Well, this is a sick man." The image of illness so disgusts the prince that he asks to be driven back to the palace.

Of course, this story goes on—the prince goes out again. On the next trip, he sees an old man, ancient, and the prince asks, "Is this coming to me? Is this coming to all?" The charioteer nods yes. Again, the prince is revolted. "How can anyone then enjoy life? How can there be delight in this life? I want to go back to the palace."

Of course, he doesn't stay there. He goes out one more time, and this time he sees a funeral, a dead man, and he learns about death.

Today we call this a trauma; he has had a traumatic experience. In our own literature the man who seems to me to represent this kind of transformative shock is Herman Melville. Brought up in lovely upper New York State in a well-to-do agrarian environment—when his father dies he is a youngster, so he goes down to New York to be with an uncle. The uncle gets the boy a job on a schooner that takes him to Liverpool, and suddenly the suffering, the sickness, the agony, the degradation of life strike him—and you know how Melville was the rest of his life.

So the Buddha-to-be looks at this corpse; he is struck by the split between the beautiful surface of things and the sense of the evil, the horror, the ruthlessness of life underneath.

He goes out on one more excursion and he sees a holy man. "Who is this?" he asks. He is told, "This is a holy man. This is a man who has gone forth to seek the answer to the riddles and pains and sorrows of the world." So the prince says, "I am going to become a holy man."

Then there comes a very important and interesting episode. He is so unhappy that his dancing girls and music girls set about entertaining their young prince, and the gods see to it that they should all fall asleep in very untidy postures. And he suddenly sees them as aged and sick and dead—this is known as the Graveyard Vision. This is what Melville experienced, the immanence, the presence of death and decay and degradation in the picture world of life.

So the prince gets up quietly and goes out to the stables and says to his charioteer, "I am going. Fix up the horse, we are off." And out they go. The divinities of the Earth cushion the horse's hooves so that they should make no clatter on the palace's cobblestones, so that no one should know that their prince was departing. Now, the prince's little boy, his son, named Impediment, has just been born. Yet Siddhārtha leaves his wife and his child and the horse goes out of the city. The goddess of the city opens the gates by magic. He is gone and the horse leaps across the river and he now is in the forest. He takes his princely sword and cuts off his lordly topknot. This is the death to the world, the death to his vocation, the death to his place in society, the death to *dharma,* the death to duty, the death to that thing that was so important to the Hindus: *dharma* is left behind.

The horse came back to the palace without his master. It returned, riderless, and died of sorrow. Now that motif, the horse without a rider, is a motif that is familiar to our culture from the funeral of John F. Kennedy. It is an Indo-European motif.

The horseless rider is the mere body without the directing spirit. It has lost its master; the master has gone to the higher spheres. The funeral of John Kennedy recapitulates symbols that stretched way back; the horse without a rider was one.

Having cut himself off from the duties that have defined his life, Siddhārtha goes from one hermit grove to another. The Buddhists are really quite cynical about the Hindu austerities; he sees these hermit groves and the crazy things these yogis are doing, and as he sees each, the young man says, "This is not the way to achieve illumination."

He goes from one teacher to another. Finally, he comes to a grove where there are five saintly men starving themselves. So he too starved himself—perhaps you have seen the Indian figures of the Buddha looking like a skeleton. He says, "I have starved myself to such an extent that when I touch my belly, I can grab my backbone. Not in this condition can one achieve illumination."

This moment is the counterpart of Christ going to John the Baptist. John the Baptist was the greatest prophet of the apocalyptic movement of his day—a Jewish yogi. Jesus goes to him, is baptized by him, and then goes past him into the solitude of the desert. There he is tempted by Satan, you remember, and transcends those temptations and then comes back himself to teach.

So, also, the future Buddha—not yet is he "the Illuminated One," for that is what *Buddha* means—learns what he can from the teachers of the world and then goes forth himself into his own meditations. He leaves his ascetic friends and sits under a tree, and this lovely girl comes to him. She is the daughter of the local herder, a very wealthy herder. She had known that she was going to bring the Buddha-to-be the refreshment that would restore his health. So she had taken the milk of a thousand cows and fed it to a hundred cows, and taken the milk of the hundred cows and fed it to ten cows, and taken the milk of the ten cows and fed it to one cow, and taken that milk and made milk-rice of it and brought it to the Buddha. So in this was concentrated all the power of all these cows. She brings this to him in a golden bowl; he eats it and is restored. When he goes to give her back the bowl, she says, "I don't take back what I have given."

So Siddhārtha tosses the bowl into a stream and says, "If the bowl goes upstream instead of down, I shall achieve illumination." And of course it goes upstream. He is going to move upstream against the stream of life to the source point from which life comes and he is going to break past even *that.*

Now, to say a word about that point, back to which the Buddha is going. In the Bṛhadāraṇyaka Upaniṣad, one of the great Hindu texts, there is a story of the Being of Beings. He was all that there was. And one moment he says the word "*ahaṃ*"—that is, "I." This was the beginning of the creation of the world. And no sooner did he say "I"—that is to say, no sooner had he defined and delineated himself—then he was afraid. Fear is the first response to being something, to imagining yourself; the psychology of I brings about the psychology of fear. Then he reasoned and he thought, What should I be afraid of since there is no one in the world but me? Of course, having realized that, he wished that there were someone else in the world. So now comes desire. First fear and then desire come right out of having said "I." And what did he do? He swelled up, split in half, became male and female, and begot the world. This is Plato's Myth of the Spheres—the idea that each of us is part of a sphere that split in half and when we find our true love, our true spouse, we recompose our original wholeness. Only the Upaniṣad tells that story on the cosmic scale. That is the mysticism of this mystery.

Now, Hinduism is a psychological religion. This is the psychology of the world coming into being. This Being of Beings said "I" and voilà! This world sprung into being. Siddhārtha wants to go backward through that same "I," out of the dualistic world of "I" and "thou," into the world of "thou art that."

Like Hinduism (and unlike the Western faiths), Buddhism is basically a psychological religion. The word *Buddhism* comes from the Sanskrit root *bodh,* which means "to illuminate," and Buddha simply means, as I have said, "the Illuminated One," or, more literally, "the One Who Is Awake." That is what Siddhārtha wants to do. He is going to go back upstream, out of the dualistic world into the transcendent world of undifferentiated *nirvāṇa.* The first and only exercise, then, was to erase the sense of "I."

How are we going to do that? That is Siddhārtha's problem here; he decides to go somewhere to have a sit and think about it. The almost-Buddha comes to a tree, the Bodhi Tree, the Tree of Illumination, that stands at what is called the Immovable Spot—T. S. Eliot's "still point of the turning world."[52] What does that mean? It is that spot in the psyche that is not moved by fear or desire. Yet it is pictured as though it were a geographical spot in the center of the world.

Siddhārtha stands on the northern side of the tree, and the whole world tips like a great wagon wheel, and he says, "This is not it, this is the unsteady place." Then he walks to the west, and the same thing happens. Then he heads to the south—the same thing. Finally he goes to the east, and everything stays set.

Now this eastern position is the position from which you see the sunrise of the new day. This is the position from which you see the new illumination. In the same way, the door to a Navajo hogan always faces east. It is with this same idea in mind that the Christian week is celebrated on Sunday, the beginning of the week. Sunday, the day of the Sun, represents the new law, the new day, the new illumination. The Hebrew celebration on Saturday—Saturn's day—represents the old day. That is exactly why the day was shifted from Saturday to Sunday. Saturn is the planet of heaviness, of weight, of obstacle, of the law, and now we are going to break past that. Similarly, in the Buddha's transcendence, the law, the *dharma* of Hinduism, is to be broken past. These are exactly equivalent concepts.

Seated there at the foot of the tree, Siddhārtha is confronted by the tempter—just like Jesus in the desert. And who is the tempter? He is that divinity who first said "I." The Lord of the World by whom all things are moved stands before the Buddha in two forms—first one, then another. This is called the Temptation of Kāma-Māra, and we will see why.

The first form the tempter takes is that of the Lord of Desire, called Kāma. And he parades before the Buddha his three beautiful daughters, whose names are Longing, Fulfillment, and Regret. Future, present, past. Well, the Buddha isn't moved because he isn't *there*. He has already disengaged himself from his ego life and identified himself with pure consciousness; he has no sense of "I." Therefore, he has no sense of "they." There is no one here. There is no one there.

This is very disappointing to the girls. We have no report of their comments, but their father, Kāma, transformed himself then into the Lord of Death, who is called Māra. *Kāma, māra,* desire and death, lust and fear. As my late friend Heinrich Zimmer used to say, "Desire is the bait, death is the hook." Death can't touch you if there is nothing you desire. So now the Lord of "I" presents himself to the Buddha in the aspect of Māra, who has a horrendous face, with tusks, and a necklace of seventy-two skulls and with weapons in his many hands. And with his army of monsters, Māra attacks the Buddha seated there at the foot of the tree. They throw at him all kinds of things. Unfortunately for them, there is nobody there, so when these weapons reach this field of nobody being there, they are transformed into bouquets of adoration.

Finally, the attacker transforms himself into Dharma, the Lord of Duty. These are the three things by which we are bound: desire, as Freud tells us; fear and aggression, as Adler and Nietzsche tell us; and duty, as our clergymen and social scientists tell us. These are the bonds from which the Buddha is breaking. The tempter, as the Lord Dharma, says, "What are you doing sitting here? Why are you not at your work, which is that of being a prince and governing?" And the Buddha simply touches the Earth with his hand—you have seen this pose in Buddha images—and the Earth herself, the Goddess World, the all-encircling universe, calls out, "This is my beloved son who through many, many lives has given, given, given of himself without thought, and he is eligible of this position."

Then the elephant on which the Lord Dharma is seated bows before the Buddha, the army disperses and, as dawn rises on the new day, the Buddha achieves illumination. This illumination so stuns him—it is an opening of the world—that he sits there for seven days. Then he steps away and for seven days, regards the spot where he had sat. Then for seven days he walks back and forth integrating what he has learned. Then he goes and sits beneath a tree and he thinks, This cannot be taught. And that is the first doctrine of Buddhism: it cannot be taught. No experience can be taught. All that can be taught is the way to an experience. Hence the essence of Buddhism is something that is implicit in ourselves and is to be achieved through experience; it cannot be delivered to us like a package. No sooner does he have this illumination than the deities themselves—Indra and Brahmā, the lords of the old Vedic pantheon—come down and they say, "Teach."

So he says, "For the good of man and the gods, I will teach." But what he teaches is not Buddhism. What he teaches is the way to Buddhism, and it is called the Middle Way. It is the way between any pair of opposites you want to think of. The first pair of opposites is of course that of extreme austerity and world negation and the extreme affirmation and luxury. It is the way between these that he chose, you remember—he ate food before his illumination. Buddhism then is a whole constellation of ways, and in Buddhism each way is called a *yāna,* a ferryboat. It is the ferryboat to the yonder shore, the shore beyond this shore, where the pairs of opposites assail us and hold us, of desire/fear, of birth/death, of liking/not liking, of doing/not doing, of people fighting each other. This is the way the world is; it cannot be otherwise. Now if you can't take it, as the Buddha as a youth could not, how are you going to get past it?

The way in which the main doctrine of Buddhism is formulated parallels the way in which an Indian medical man is supposed to diagnose a disease, according to the authoritative texts. First he asks, What is the disease? What is the matter here? That is the first noble question and the First Noble Truth in answer is, "All life is sorrowful." Remember the sorrows that Siddhārtha saw as a young man: disease, old age, and death. The second question the doctor has to ask is, Can this disease be cured? There is no use going to work unless it can be cured. The Second Noble Truth, in response to this question, is that indeed, the disease can be cured. There is release from this round of sorrows. The third question is, What is health? What is it that we are trying to achieve? What we are trying to achieve through the practice of Buddhism is the release from sorrow that is *nirvāṇa.* As we have seen, the word *nirvāṇa* means "extinguished." Literally, however, the word is translated as "where no wind blows," or "beyond the winds." Buddhism is the ferry way to the yonder shore, where the wind of surface duality does not blow. We leave this shore of fear, of desire, etc.; we get in the ferryboat of the Buddhist *yāna,* the Buddhist vessel, and we come to the yonder shore where there are no pairs of opposites, so that the ultimate realization is: now we are on the yonder shore, we look back to see this shore, since we are beyond the pairs of opposites, and surprise! There is no difference. This world is *nirvāṇa;* that is the point. As the Gnostic Gospel According to Thomas says, "The Kingdom of the Father is spread upon the Earth, and men do not see it."[53]

The message of the Buddha is simple but profound: we are to seek joyful participation in the suffering of the world.

In the West, this paradox is explored through the image of the Crucifixion. There are two ways of rendering the Crucifixion. One is the more popular way, with Christ there bleeding and suffering, the man of sorrow.

But there is another way that's called Christ Triumphant, and there you see the Christ on the cross, eyes open, head erect, wearing a tunic. He has come willingly and there is no suffering: joyful participation in the suffering. These are two totally different renditions of the Crucifixion. One expresses, you might say, the master spirit; the other expresses the slave spirit. Buddhism is more the master spirit all the way through.

The lives and myths of the Buddha and Christ make for a very interesting comparison. Particularly, it fascinates me to look at how their stories express the different ideas of Occident and Orient with regard to life and rebirth.

Now, in the West—both the Levant and Europe—the seasons are relatively extreme; the passage of the seasons is a major motif in myth and art. So you have an emphasis on time and death and resurrection rather than reincarnation. And it's in that context that the dead and resurrected god is a very important deity. This goes way, way back to very ancient times. You find it in Mesopotamia with Tammuz, the one who dies and is resurrected. In Egypt, this is the story cycle of Osiris; in Greece, it is Adonis. And of course, we find this myth in the Gospels as well. They are all associated with lunar powers. Always, their rebirth is associated with the full Moon near the vernal equinox.

Then in India, you are in a tropical, jungle zone, and as Goethe says when he talks about the Sanskrit dramatic masterpiece *Śakuntalā Recognized,* "There you have the blossom and the fruit at the same time." The seasons don't mean too much; time seems to be just the same time, all the time. Here there is an accent on the stillness. So in Europe what you have in the imagery of the savior is an accent on the passing time; the crisis of threshold of death and rebirth. But in the Buddhist thing, the accent is on the still point. When the Buddha drops his hand and quits the world, you know, that is the counterpart of the Crucifixion. That is leaving the world to go to the Father, though he is doing it psychologically rather than corporeally. He leaves the world of the body; he drops it. Then he comes back bestowing the boon of his newly gained wisdom—that's the counterpart of the Resurrection on Easter Sunday. Easter Sunday is the counterpart of the Buddha's *paranirvāṇa.* And the Buddha touching the Earth is the counterpart of the Crucifixion. But you see what's happening. In the West, the agony aspect has been accented, you see. In Buddhism it is not.

Now, when you have the Bodhisattvas, such as Amitābha, willingly coming back to the world—that's where Christ comes into closer connection. The Bodhisattva embraces joyful participation in the sorrows of the world. If you want a vivid representation of joyful participation in the sorrows of the world, Christ crucified and triumphant is it. We read in Paul's Epistle to the Philippians that wonderful passage: "Let this mind be in you, which was also in Christ Jesus/Who, being in the form of God, thought it not robbery to be equal with God/But made himself of no reputation, and took upon him the form of a servant, and was made in the likeness of men/And being found in fashion as a man, he humbled himself, and became obedient unto death, even the death of the cross".[54] That is, out of love for the world, he came into it, joyfully participating in its sorrows. And that means suffering the sorrows yourself. They glue together very well. But the essential difference between the authorized traditions is the unique godhood of Christ: we do not participate in it—only by imitation.

In Buddhism, we are all Buddha beings, and the only problem is that we don't know it; we don't act as though we were.

Mahāvīra, as I have pointed out, was a contemporary of the Buddha and the Buddha despised the Jainist doctrine of material asceticism. He said that this idea of a purely physical detachment from the world is altogether wrong in its thinking. The proper problem is psychological.

The Buddha came forward with this idea around 500 B.C. This was a moment of immense importance. It does not matter whether you eat meat, said Siddhārtha Gautama Śākyamuni. It does not matter whether you kill things as you walk around. What matters is your psychological attitude. Do you act with desire for the fruits of action or with fear, or do you act simply because it is your duty to act? This is known in Buddhism as *karma yoga*—acting without desire or fear, but simply in terms of the process.

Ferryboats

There are a number of *yānas,* these different Buddhist paths to enlightenment. Where do they come from? Think of them as the different ferryboat docks from which people may set forth. One can think of this world, let's say, as the Atlantic Coast of North America. Well, there are lots of ports from which you can set forth to the yonder shore. There is Halifax. There is Boston. There is New York. There is Baltimore. Each of these could be called a Buddha realm, a certain mode, a certain attitude characteristic of the particular psychological type that is suited to a particular starting place. A New Englander wouldn't feel comfortable launching from Maryland, nor would a New Yorker choose Nova Scotia as a starting point.

The first way, the way known as Theravāda, is the monastic movement that I mentioned in relation to the Jains. It is also known as the Hinayāna, the "little ferryboat," since it is the way of monastic asceticism.[55] Little ferryboat Buddhism is the Buddhism of monks, the Buddhism of people who make a distinction between this shore and that and are striving to get there. They have to give up the world, they have to give up their families, as Christians do who go into a convent or become Trappist monks. They change their names—they are somebody else entirely.

The followers of this way say, "Yes, all life is sorrowful and we are going to leave it now. We are going into the forest, to be monks in our solitude—how happy are we. The world drops off behind us, and fare thee well; that is the world of fools." That is why this is called the little ferryboat—it is for the few who are willing to go across to the yonder shore to stay. This was the first Buddhism, but it survives today in Ceylon, and in Southeast Asia.

But when you get to the yonder shore and realize that this world is it, what are your ways to be? The next Buddhist way is called the Mahāyāna, which means the "great ferryboat." This is meant to be the boat on which we all can ride—it takes us to the yonder shore and then ferries us back to this world. There is, in this tradition, a great figure named Avalokiteśvara, also called Kuan-yin in China or Kannon in Japan. This is the archetypal Bodhisattva, the one whose being *(sattva)* is illumination *(bodhi)* but who has not departed from the world. He (or, sometimes she) is always represented with a tiara, a crown of kingly rule, addressing himself to the world.

Avalokiteśvara, on the point of illumination, heard the whole world cry out, "If you leave us we shall have lost our experience of the presence of *nirvāṇa.*" So he remained in the world; he did not leave it. For this he is known as the Listening One. And all of us are aspects you might say of Avalokiteśvara, this Bodhisattva, this knower, this teacher, insofar as in our intercourse with each other we are illuminating each other; we are operating in his manner, so to say.

We see images of this great Boddhisattva throughout the Far East in the lovely figure of Kwan-yin looking down in mercy on the world. That principle of mercy engages us in the world, addressing ourselves to others with sympathy, with compassion for their sense of sorrow. We feel the world is sorrowful. We see people feeling that they are in sorrow and yet they are actually in delight. The truth is that since this is *nirvāṇa,* we are all motivated by delight, and so we are. So life is.

There is a great Buddhist text, the Prajñāpāramitā Sūtra, and it's only a very short, concise thing of about a page and a half, and it culminates in one line, which is to be the summary of the whole sense of Mahāyāna Buddhism. That line goes like this: *Aum gottam, Buddha-tam, pariqatam, pārasangatam. Bodhi!* "Gone, gone, gone to the yonder shore, landed on the yonder shore, illumination!" Hallelujah.

That is the summary of the whole thing. *Prajñāpāramitā:* The wisdom of the yonder shore, beyond pairs of opposites. The one who is trying to get away from life to *nirvāṇa* is still caught in pairs of opposites. But when you get there, you realize that this is it right now.

There is another figure who is very important, and this is Amida, or Amitābha. We met him in the Bardo Thödol. *Amitā* means "immeasureable" and *bha* means "radiance." So Amitābha is the Buddha of Immeasurable Radiance. This is a variety of Buddhism that seems to have come into being around the second or third centuries A.D. in northern India, and it went from there to China and Japan. This potential Buddha on the point of illumination took a vow. He said, "Let me not achieve Buddhahood unless through my achievement I can bring all beings to *nirvāṇa* simply by mentioning or thinking my name!" And indeed, when he did become illuminated there sprang forth before him a great pond. This is known as Sukhāvatī, the realm of bliss, the realm of delight, and on this pond are many lotuses.

The individual who thinks of Amida will on death not be reincarnated back into the world but will find himself seated in a lotus; he will be in one of those lotuses. If he has lived a very bad life but nevertheless has thought now and then about Amida, the lotus will be closed and will stay closed for quite a long while. If he has lived a spiritual life, the lotus may be almost open. In any case, presently the lotus will open, but what makes it open? Here are all these lotuses on this wonderful lake. The Buddha himself is seated there. This is the Buddha whose image you will see in the shrines of China, Japan, and many of the shrines of ancient India. His Sun-like radiance is penetrating those lotuses with illumination. Just remember, *bodh* means "illuminated." The illumination is pouring in, and the waters are of five colors, just as we are all made up of five elements. And they are rippling with a certain song; the waters sing the great Buddhist doctrine, "All is impermanent. All is without a self." This is the basic meditation of Buddhism.

The image is given of the light of a candle. Is that the same light now that was there a second before? Heraclitus said we do not step out of the same river that we stepped into. So also our bodies are constantly changing; all the cells in your body change. Is there a continuity of anything but recollection?

The basic thought of Buddhism is that there is nobody there; there is nobody to save. This image of man is just a reflection, based on the activity of your mind. It is an illusion. You say yes to the illusion. Sure, because it is the same thing as the nonbeing. It is not in being. The wonderful Heart Sūtra says, "Form is emptiness, and the very emptiness is form." The world is *nirvāṇa, nirvāṇa* is the world. So don't be anxious. Nothing is happening. Get into the spirit of this rippling play with its joys, with its sorrows, with its horrors. But at the same time, be aware that there is this void beneath *(śūnyatā)*, the full void, the void that makes you one with all things that are no things.

And so in this form of Buddhism we have simply what is called *bhakti,* or devotion; no thinking necessary. Remember, the Buddha went through great austerities. The Buddha went through great ordeals. But here is an easy Buddhism. This is the popular Buddhism. This is the Buddhism that corresponds to that mode of popular worship that in India is associated with devotion to the gods. One prays to the Buddha knowing that that

Buddha is really not there because there is no being, that Buddha is a reflection of one's own potential Buddhahood. And in meditating on him, clinging to him, one is gradually losing attachment to one's little ego world.

You are, as we say in the Christian tradition, "resting in God." You relax. You turn yourself over to the divinity. You turn yourself over to the mystery with the confidence that that mystery will support you without your knowing why or how, without your being illuminated within, but simply assuming the posture of one who is illuminated, acting as though you knew that you weren't anything. That is the great Amida Buddha.

This Buddhism comes to Japan in the twelfth century with the great teacher Hōnen and becomes the basis for the great Buddhism of most of the people of Japan now, Jōdo and Shinshū.

Now, how do you serve that Buddha? How do you launch your ferry-boat across to the yonder shore? You serve that Buddha simply by performing your life duties. No meditations necessary. No special going to church necessary. Your whole life is a church. Your children are your enterprise through which you achieve your fulfillment. This is a lovely, wonderful thing. The whole world is turned into the sanctuary, you might say, of the discipline. And the discipline isn't something that should make you anxious. It is something that you are doing simply by performing your life duties properly and peacefully.

Now there comes a resistance to this kind of thing on the part of people who like effort. You know, there are people who feel things shouldn't be too easy, and this way of high discipline is the way that is epitomized in what is called Zen. This word *zen* is the Japanese pronunciation of the Chinese word *ch'an,* and the Chinese word is a mispronunciation of the Sanskrit word *dhyāna,* which means "contemplation." Contemplation normally is thought of as disciplined meditation. I have spoken about the *kuṇḍalinī* yoga, a form of psychological and spiritual discipline that consists of bringing a serpent of energy up through the spine. In Zen, you seek to transform your mode of experience through just this kind of spiritual exercise so that you actually come to the illumination that the Buddha came to in the way that the Buddha himself did, not just seated in a shrine being a little dragon mouth saying, "Buddha, Buddha, Buddha," then expecting to get somewhere. Here you are going to go to *work.*

This way of contemplation goes from India, where contemplation is an old, old story, to China. Buddhism enters China about the first century A.D.—A.D. 67 is the year usually given. Then for about five hundred years, the Chinese Buddhists were engaged in the translation of texts from Sanskrit into Chinese. People became very much interested—as religious people very often do—in details of cult, of ritual discipline, of the interpretation of words, and all that kind of thing. Then an Indian Buddhist named Bodhidharma came to China and he sat facing a wall for nine years and didn't say a darn word.

The point here was that one achieves Buddhahood through the illumination of the mind, not through a proper reading of a text, nor through the proper performance of a ritual. Illumination comes from having something happening inside. Meditation, *dhyāna,* is the main exercise. This is the beginning of Zen, exactly the contrary discipline to that of Amida Buddhism, where we sit with rituals and incense and lights and images. In Bodhidharma's Buddhism, you don't need these rituals and outer trappings anymore. This is the way of the disciplined mind.

Well this isn't very congenial to the Chinese. Perhaps you know the Chinese spirit? Oswald Spengler, in his review of world history, *The Decline of the West,* calls theirs a culture of wandering spirit.

So the Chinese struggled with this form of Buddhism. Now, we get the legend of the wonderful Hui-neng, circa A.D. 713. It is with Hui-neng that Buddhism becomes East Asian, not Indian. Again, the story is legendary but it is given always as a true story. A farm boy whose father had died is supporting his mother by carrying wood around and delivering it to people's houses. One day, he was waiting for somebody to answer the door when he heard somebody reciting the Heart Sūtra. He heard, "All is emptiness, the very form is emptiness; no self, no being, no clouds, no world," and he got it.

So then he goes to a monastery, leaving his mother and all behind. Well, he can't even read Chinese let alone Sanskrit, so he is put to work in the kitchen.

The young monks are under the discipline of an abbot, and the abbot is getting pretty old; it is time for him to retire. And so he sets up a little contest: anyone who can write four verses summing up Buddhism and give the most elucidating exposition of Buddhism will be the next abbot. So there was a young man in the monastery that everybody knew was going to be the great one, and he wrote on the wall:

> The body is the tree of illumination,
> The mind is a mirror bright,
> The mind is a mirror through which illumination is achieved.
> Always keep it dusted clean lest dust on it alight.

Hui-neng comes out from the kitchen and asks his friend to read him that, and the friend reads it, and he says, "Now write this":

> The body is not the Bodhi Tree.
> The mind no mirror bright.
> Since nothing is there,
> On what should dust alight?[56]

Well, this is really one step closer to the ultimate doctrine. When the abbot came down the next morning, all the monks were jabber, jabber, jabbering. No one knew who had written that on the wall. And the abbot pretended to be very angry, and he took his slipper and wiped it off. The young monks went through their day. Then that evening the abbot calls Hui-neng to him and says, "Come up here. Here are the robes of office. Here is the begging bowl of the patriarch. Go away."

What would happen to the discipline of all these young monks if their religion should be broken up like this with ultimate illumination? They are not ready for it yet. The point here is, you are not supposed simply to sit; that is not what it is all about. Walk around. So this is the illumination of walking around as you live, the enlightenment you find through what you are doing.

When you read about Zen there is something rather confusing about it because this story of Hui-neng is told and told and told as the typical story of Zen. But then behind that there is Bodhidharma, the one who sat facing the wall all those years. Then go to Japan and go to a Zen monastery and what do you see? You see rows of austere little monks sitting in the most fantastically controlled meditational postures. What is all this about?

What group of people did Zen serve when it came to Japan? It was the Buddhism of the samurai, of the knights, of the warrior-monks. This gives you the clue to Zen. In contrast to the Chinese *ch'an,* Japanese Zen is the religion of knighthood, of athletes, of highly disciplined action, of being in high form. In China, the ideal is really the old rogue, the old fellow who's got wisdom in him, a kind of comical character through whom life just flows. The ideal in Japan, however, is this samurai discipline, the discipline of life in form.

When I was in Japan I went to a number of tea ceremonies that were given for me and my wife, and the first one was given in a Shinshū temple and was given to illustrate to me the difference between popular Buddhism and Zen.[57] So I am going to try to tell you what this difference was in terms as it was presented to me, namely of a tea ceremony. The tea ceremony is supposed to be conducted with great ease; yet the formality is such that if you put your teacup down here instead of there, it is as though you had gone to see the queen of England with your galoshes on. The slightest change, the slightest variation in the discipline, is something just altogether wrong. It is a faux pas.

You enter a lovely little garden and you sit on a bench, and there will be a couple of boxes out of which the tea bowls have been taken, and you examine these. When the time comes and you are called, you stroll toward the teahouse, which is a tiny little house just built for taking tea. The door through which you enter is very small, which makes entering not an easy job. Yet you have got to come in quite gracefully. This teaches humility. You are leaving something outside. That is the difficult passage. That is the entrance into a little world.

Then you come into this lovely little room that has been designed just for the tea ceremony, and the man who designed it, the tea master, will have searched the world for a pole, a post, that is the main element here, something that is natural and yet not natural—an elegant, wonderful piece of wood.

There will be a little shelf with some little knickknack on it, a little box. It has no use. It is something to regard; it is some thing. You haven't thought of anything as a thing before as a no thing. This is a kind of mystery. Then there is a hanging on the wall. One or two tiny little things are placed there that you are to regard for themselves. No great clutter, just one or two things. The whole point is everything isolated down to the essence of beauty or arrangement, and that is what you regard.

Then the tea ceremony begins. You are given little cakes to eat and you are given this wonderful, strange powdered tea. This tea is dipped into a bowl, and then the boiling water is put in with a ladle. Then it is made to foam with a little whisk that looks a little like a shaving brush made out of bamboo, and you drink this ambrosia. It is a little bit bitter, but when you get to like it, it is awfully good. Then, in certain special ways, you return the cup.

Now, the two bowls that were served to me were the things that I was to get the message from. The bowl from the popular sect, the Shinshū sect, was a lovely ceramic, kind of gray-blue with a darker blue rim; the glaze had been allowed to drip down, and it was rather thick. I would say that bowl was almost as thick as my little figure and it felt soft. You had the feeling of something substantial and vital and warm. That was the popular Buddhism. The Zen bowl, which had been made by a Zen monk, was eggshell thin and it was extremely tense. It was very dry to the touch and chafed your hand a little. It was thinly glazed in a nice dough-colored tan, and it was austere and tense—just as the tea ceremony was tense. And yet it was relaxed, because through that tension there is relaxation.

Suddenly it dawned on me—I have tested this since in one way or another—the main thing about Zen is that it asks you to have the kind of being-in-form condition of an athlete at the height of his power throughout your life and in everything you do, so that you are not in the relaxed state of living as people are at home, raising their children. You are more in the high-tension mode of life of an athlete, of a warrior. That is why judo, kendo (Japanese fencing), and *kyūdō* (archery) are all part of the way to get into the sense of Zen.

So, among the various Buddhist ferryboats, you range all the way from the sort of contemplative austerity that Bodhidharma represents to the austerity of athletic meditation-in-action that is Zen. And in between you have the lovely, warm activities of life embraced by Amida. No matter what way you choose, that is the Buddha way. Well, why do you choose this way instead of that or that way instead of another? *Because you like it.* There is no compulsion here whatsoever. The whole point is simply to realize that anything you are doing, anything you are looking at, is the opening to the way.

Now the key story for me about Buddhism concerns the sermon where the Buddha was seated, and there was a great group around him and he just held up a flower. Just a flower. One in the group *got* what the Buddha was on about. For him, the flower itself was enough to spark enlightenment. The rest of the crowd were still in the dark, so to speak, so the Buddha delivered a sermon—the great Flower Wreath Sūtra—to explain what he meant, which was this: there is nothing to say about life. It has no meaning. You make meaning. If you want a meaning in your life, find a meaning and bring it into your life, but life won't give you a meaning. Meaning is a concept. It is a notion of an end toward which you are going. The point of Buddhism is *this is it.*

The Buddha is called *tathāgata,* "the one who has come, thus"; the flower is the *tathāgata* that has come thus. The Buddha is often shown just looking at the flower. That flower is the world. That flower is a flower. That flower is what I am looking at now. This has been made to serve an end but that is not the essence of the mystery of this thing. The essence of the mystery is its very being, which has a ring around it of cosmic ocean, you might say, beyond which you cannot look.

Buddhism is the illumination to the fact, the realization of the fact that this is it. You are it and it is nothing. It is a very difficult thing to tell anyone about because the words themselves suggest that there is a meaning here, but the thing is just to get it, and that is why you can't communicate or teach Buddhism: you can only bring a person up to it.

All these different disciplines are meant simply to do that. In Japan, I met two Buddhists, a Theravāda monk from Burma and a Mahāyāna businessman—a Japanese man of the world. We were all mingling at a cocktail party. The Japanese, when I came to him, had just been hearing about monastic Buddhism. He had a glass of beer in his hand and a shrimp on a toothpick, and he said to me, "We Japanese, I think, are very funny Buddhists. We are eating, eating all the time, go right ahead, don't worry. The Japanese Mahāyāna monk, if you put meat into his bowl, he will eat the meat. It wasn't killed for him. That is the world." The other monk would not touch meat. He had all kinds of taboos, rules around his life, but the Mahāyāna takes it as it comes.

There is a fierce side to this attitude, and it comes out in war craft. You see, if everything is all right, then that is all right, too. If you are going to say yes to the world, you say yes to the world, and that is all there is to it. If your role in the world is to kill, then kill. Don't feel guilty about it. Don't feel pride about it.

There is a wonderful story about a Japanese samurai that sums this up. A samurai had spent months tracking down the man who killed his overlord. He had run the man down and now he had gotten him cornered. And he draws his samurai sword. The man's back is against the wall—he can't do a thing. In his terror and exasperation, the man against the wall spits at the samurai. The samurai puts his sword back in the sheath, turns, and walks away.

Now why did he do that? It made him angry. If he had killed that man in anger, it would have been *his* act. He would have bound himself to the world of fear and desire, wrath. Until the moment when the man had spit at him, he had been able to hold himself so that nothing was happening; now he had lost that balance. He had lost the immovable spot. He could no longer say that he was acting without acting. Anyone in athletics knows that that is the way to be an athlete. You are acting and you are not acting. The thing is taking place, and that is the way this should have happened.

So this is a religion that, in its ultimate mystery, is awfully hard to grasp. Yet it is a religion that in its actual performance is awfully easy to sympathize with and go with because anything you are doing is it. The main sin is inadvertence, not being attentive to life, to the moment you are in, to its mystery, to what is happening right here now. When that is there, and you realize that the whole mystery and void is shining through at you, you are there.

There is nothing you can say about it. And that yonder shore is this shore; we are all right there shining with all this right now.

ENVOY

The Tiger in the Depths

The Cry of the Buddha Child

There is a wonderful little story that is told about the birth of the Buddha. The Buddha was born from his mother's side, in a miraculous manner, and deities came down from heaven to receive this little child on a golden cloth, and they put him on the ground, and the first thing he did immediately after he was born was to take seven steps. Then he points up, and points down, and in a voice of thunder he says, "Worlds above, worlds beneath—there is no one in the world like me."

I heard Dr. Daisetz Suzuki, the great Zen teacher, give a little lecture on just that theme.[58] "Now, that is a very funny thing: a baby just born takes seven steps and says a thing like that," he said. "You would think he should wait until he had his second birth, his spiritual birth under the tree, but," he said, "you know we in the Orient, we are all mixed up. We don't make a distinction between spirit and matter—material birth, spiritual birth, all the same."

Then he went on, giving a long lecture, quoting *sūtras* and sacred texts, making believe to lose notes so that we could help him. You know how in Chinese pictures there are blank spaces that your imagination is to fill in so that you go into the picture. Well, so a good lecturer leaves cracks in lectures. To lecture is a little bit alienating—with the teacher and students feeling set apart from each other. So Dr. Suzuki would fumble around and mispronounce things and lose the notes so that we could all participate in the action of the teaching, so that we were all in it.

He finally said, "You know, they tell me when a baby is born, the baby cries. What does the baby say when the baby cries? The baby says, 'Worlds above, worlds beneath—there is no one in the world like me.'"

"Now," he said, "all babies are Buddha babies. So what's the difference between Queen Māya's baby and your baby? That one *knew* it was a Buddha baby and he behaved out of that knowledge. Yours is still caught in the toils of sense and mistake and the wrong instruction we're all giving it and all that kind of thing, and it has to break through. But this one, he had lived enough lifetimes that when he came down for his last look at things, to render in his life the image of a life lived, he was yoked to pure consciousness."

So what you are yoking yourself to is Buddhahood, not the Buddha. Consequently, for the Buddhists, it doesn't matter whether the Buddha actually lived or not—one need not have faith in his life as a historical fact, as a Christian is supposed to believe of Christ. For the Christian it makes a difference whether the savior did actually live, but not for the Buddhist. The Buddha, whether he is a mythological image or a fact, is a rendition of the mystery of Buddhahood in life, and he doesn't have to have been there at all for you to find the Buddhahood in yourself. He can serve just as a mythological figure, as a shadow on the wall, as an inspiration to you to find it in yourself, and then you are in. You become one with the eternal, the source of being.

The Tigers and the Goats

To conclude, let me just tell a little Indian animal story. Their stories are wonderful, and they illuminate things in the snap of the fingers. This particular fable was a favorite of Ramakrishna.

Once there was a she-tiger who was pregnant and starving. She came upon a little herd of goats, and in her zeal, she pounced too hard. The goats scattered, she landed flat, brought on the birth of her little one, and died herself. The goats came back to where they had been, and they had very strong parental instincts. They saw this tiny little just-born tiger with its dead mother, and they adopted it.

The tiger grew up thinking it was a goat. It learned to eat grass, it learned to bleat. It couldn't see itself in a mirror, so it didn't know that it wasn't a goat. Of course, neither grass nor bleating is natural for tigers, and so it was a pretty miserable specimen of its kind by the time it reached adolescence.

Then, one day, a great big male tiger who was out hunting pounced at the same little herd, and again the goats scattered. But the young orphan was, after all, a tiger, and he stood there, facing the invader down.

The big fellow looked at him in astonishment, and he said, "What are you doing, living here with goats?"

"Baa," said the younger tiger, and he nibbled at a bit of grass.

Well, the big boy was mortified—what a shock to find a member of his species in this condition! He gave the young one a buffet or two and got only these silly bleats. In desperation he picked the little one up by the scruff of the neck and took him to a quiet pond.

Now, as I have said, the idea of yoga is that the rippling of the mind should stand still and be like a quiet pond, and then you will see the perfect image. So the little fellow looked into the quiet pond. The big fellow, the guru, looked in, too. The guru said, "Look at my face. Look at yours. You have got the pot face of a tiger. You are not a goat. You are like me: be like me."

The little one gave another silly bleat, but something is sinking in.

Again he was picked up by the neck. This time he was taken to the tiger's den, where there was a recently killed gazelle, all bloody and nice and yummy. The big fellow took a big chunk of this stuff and shoved it at the little one.

The little one backed away in disgust: "I'm a vegetarian."

"Come on, now," said the big one, and he shoved this bloody stuff down his throat. The little one gagged on it. "So," Ramakrishna says at this point, "all do on true doctrine." He gagged, all right, but it got into his veins, and he began to feel something going buzzing along that he had never felt before—the right food.

Spontaneously, his own tiger nature got hold of him, and, without even knowing it, he gave a tiger stretch, and something that wasn't quite a roar, but it was enough for the big fellow who knew roars to recognize it as a possibility.

The big fellow said, "There we are now. Now we go into the forest and eat tiger food."

I like this story, and I tell it to my students, and when I ask them what the moral is, the answer I get is, "Put a tiger in your tank." So this is what the story tells us: we are all tigers living among these goats. So go into the forest, and in the forest of the night, find the tiger burning bright in your own profound depths.

CHAPTER NOTES

INTRODUCTION

1. This introduction is drawn from the beginning of a lecture entitled "Transformation of Myth Through Time." (L1022), delivered in Santa Fe, New Mexico, on 9 November, 1982; the remainder of the lecture was released as "From God to Goddess," episode 4 of *The Shaping of Our Mythic Tradition,* vol. 1 of the video series *Mythos.*
2. For an exploration of Carl Gustav Jung's theories of the archetypes of the collective unconscious, theories that were central to Campbell's own ideas, see *Mythos: The Shaping of Our Mythic Tradition,* episode 1, "Psyche and Symbol" (Los Angeles: Inner Dimension, 1996). See also C. G. Jung, *The Portable Jung,* ed. Joseph Campbell, "The Concept of the Collective Unconscious" (New York: Viking Press, 1971).
3. Chief Seattle was a leader of the Suquamish tribe on the edge of the Puget Sound, near the site of the city that would one day bear his name. In 1854, when the American government offered to buy the land of his tribe, Seattle delivered an oration that included the statement, "This we know: the Earth does not belong to Man; Man belongs to the Earth." There are several transcriptions of the speech, all edited and filtered through the

Western consciousness; yet the speech remains a remarkable expression of a pre-Western view of the relationship of humanity to nature.

4. Campbell purchased this television in 1963 when he appeared on New York public television in a series of lectures entitled "Mask, Myth and Dream."
5. Immanuel Kant, *A Critique of Pure Reason,* trans. Norman Kemp Smith (New York: St. Martin's Press, 1985), p. 65.
6. See n. 3.

CHAPTER I

7. This section and the one following are drawn largely from a lecture entitled "Oriental Myth" (L382), delivered at the New School for Social Research on 3 February, 1972, which was released as "Interpreting Oriental Myth," pt. 1 of *The Eastern Way,* vol. 3 of *The Joseph Campbell Audio Collection.*
8. Martin Buber (1878–1965) was a philosopher and Jewish theologian. His best known work is *I and Thou* (New York: Touchstone Books, 1974), which explores the relationship of the self ("I") with the phenomenal universe, the objects and creatures of which may be regarded as either "it" or ""thou."
9. Gershom Scholem (1897–1982) was a noted author on Jewish mysticism and religion.
10. Campbell made the trip to which he refers in 1954–1955. His journals of this journey have been published as *Baksheesh & Brahman: Asian Journals—India* and *Sake & Satori: Asian Journals—Japan* (Novato, Calif.: New World Library, 2002).
11. Recent discoveries have established the beginning of the Bronze Age in China with the advent of the Xia dynasty, c. 2000 B.C. Campbell's point remains valid.
12. This is the basic thesis of the first title in the Collected Works of Joseph Campbell series, edited by Eugene Kennedy: *Thou Art That: Transforming Religious Metaphor* (Novato, Calif.: New World Library, 2001).
13. Gilbert Murray (1866–1957) was a prolific translator and a professor of Greek at Oxford University, in addition to campaigning for women's rights and the League of Nations. His article "Prometheus and Job"

seems to have been the source of this witticism and of Campbell's inspiration in making this comparison.

14. As of this writing, though much work is being done in the field, this script is still undeciphered.
15. For an extended discussion of the *ji-hōkai* and *ri-hōkai*, see Campbell's journals of his 1955 journey to Japan, *Sake & Satori*, pp. 96–99.
16. This section is drawn from the later part a lecture entitled "Oriental Myth" (L382), delivered at the New School for Social Research on 3 February, 1972, which was released as "Interpreting Oriental Myth," pt. 1 of *The Eastern Way*, vol. 3 of *The Joseph Campbell Audio Collection*, and from part 3 of a November, 1957 lecture that Campbell gave to the Foreign Service Institute entitled "Main Themes in Indian Philosophy" (L24).
17. For more discussion of this topic, see *Thou Art That*, pp. 89–90, 113.
18. Song ascribed to Candidasa (c. fifteenth century), a Balinese songwriter; translation based on Shashibhusan Dasgupta, *Obscure Religious Cults As Background of Bengali Literature* (Calcutta: University of Calcutta, 1946), p. 137.

CHAPTER II

19. This chapter and the one following are drawn largely from the second part of a series entitled "Symbolism and Mystical Experience" (L121), delivered at Wainwright House on 17 October, 1966, which was released as "The Mystical Tradition in India," pt. 3 of *The Eastern Way*, vol. 3 of *The Joseph Campbell Audio Collection*. The section in which Campbell compares the imagery of yoga and of psychosis is drawn from a lecture entitled "Yoga" (L245), which was delivered on 26 February 1969 at Cooper Union. The section concerning Kṛṣṇa and the gopīs comes from an unpublished article fragment (I54) that may have been cut from *Oriental Mythology*, vol. 2 of *The Masks of God* (New York: Viking, 1962). Several segments of the section entitled "Yoga of the Body, Mind, and Heart" are drawn from the unpublished article fragment, "Erotic Yoga" (I38).
20. Campbell explores this idea in several books, including *Sake & Satori*, p. 146; *Oriental Mythology*, pp. 294–95; and *Occidental Mythology*, vol. 3 of *The Masks of God* (New York: Viking, 1964), pp. 285–86, 362.
21. For Campbell's most thorough reviews of the imagery of *kuṇḍalinī*

yoga, see *The Inner Reaches of Outer Space: Metaphor As Myth and As Religion* (Novato, Calif.: New World Library, 2002), pp. 35–45, or *The Mythic Image,* Bollingen Series C (Princeton, N.J.: Princeton University Press, 1974), "The Lotus Ladder," pp. 330–91.

22. R. D. Laing, *The Politics of Experience* (London: Penguin Books, 1967).
23. Swami Nikhilananda, trans., *The Gospel of Sri Ramakrishna,* ed. Joseph Campbell (New York: Ramakrishna-Vivekananda Center, 1942), p. 242.
24. William Wordsworth, "Lines Completed a Few Miles above Tintern Abbey," ll. 98–102.
25. The Gospel According to Saint John, 1:1.
26. Saraha, *Dohakosa,* ed. P. C. Bagchi, nos. 47, 48, translation based on Shashibhusan Dasgupta, *Obscure Religious Cults As Background of Bengali Literature* (University of Calcutta, 1946), p. 104.
27. Dasgupta, *Obscure Religious Cults,* pp. 58–59.
28. Ibid., p. 158.
29. Arthur Schopenhauer *The World as Will and Representation (Die Welt als Wille und Vorstellung),* trans. E. F. J. Payne (New York: Dover Publications, 1966).
30. Nikhilananda, *Gospel of Sri Ramakrishna.*
31. This story was adapted from Sister Nivedita (Margaret E. Nobel) and Ananda K. Coomaraswamy, *Myths of the Hindus and Buddhists* (New York: Dover Publications, 1967), pp. 228–35.
32. This section and the one preceding are drawn largely from the second part of a series entitled "Symbolism and Mystical Experience" (L121), delivered at Wainwright House on 17 October, 1966, which was released as "The Mystical Tradition in India," pt. 3 of *The Eastern Way,* vol. 3 of *The Joseph Campbell Audio Collection.*
33. This section is drawn from a lecture entitled "World Soul," pt. 2 of a series entitled "Art and Religion of India," delivered at the Asia Society in 1968, which was also released as *The World Soul,* in *The Inward Journey—East and West,* vol. 2 of *The Joseph Campbell Audio Collection.*
34. The Book of Genesis, 1:1–3.
35. Gottfried von Strassburg, *Tristan,* trans. A. T. Hatto (New York: Viking Press, 1960), p. xxx.
36. This section is based on a lecture entitled "Oriental Concepts of the Individual" (L43), delivered on 20 February 1961 as part of a series at The

Cooper Union Forum titled Influences and Concepts. This lecture has not been released in audio format due to poor sound quality of the recording.

37. The *personae* complex is one of the psychological structures that Jung referred to as archetypes. For more information on the archetypes of the collective unconconsious, see n. 2.
38. This section is drawn from the lecture "Imagery of Rebirth Yoga: The Tibetan Book of the Dead" (L243), delivered at Beloit College in January 1969, which was also released as "Imagery of Rebirth Yoga," pt. 4 of *The Inward Journey—East and West,* vol. 2 of *The Joseph Campbell Audio Collection.*
39. Kazi Dawa-Samdup, trans., *The Tibetan Book of the Dead,* comp., ed. W. Y. Evans-Wentz, 3d ed. (London: Oxford University Press, 1960).
40. This meeting is documented in Joseph Campbell's journal of his 1955 journey to India, *Baksheesh & Brahman: Asian Journals—India* (Novato, Calif.: New World Library, 2002), pp. 277–79.
41. This section is drawn from the lecture "Philosophical Concepts of Creativity in the Orient" (L191), delivered at The Cooper Union and broadcast over WNYC Radio on 31 January 1968, which was released as "Creativity in Oriental Myth," pt. 5 of *The Eastern Way,* vol. 3 of *The Joseph Campbell Audio Collection.*
42. Joseph Needham, *Science and Civilisation in China,* vol. 2, *History of Scientific Thought* (Cambridge: Cambridge University Press, 1956).
43. Ananda K. Coomaraswamy, *The Transformation of Nature in Art* (New York: Dover Publications, 1956), p. 64.
44. Campbell was a close friend of Western writer on Zen and the Tao Alan Watts. Through Watts, he knew of Jack Kerouac, Neal Cassady, and Gary Snyder, the beatnik *dharma* bums who explored Zen as a path to spontaneous creativity and enlightenment. Their exploits were chronicled in several of Kerouac's novels, most famously in *The Dharma Bums* (New York: Viking Press, 1958).

CHAPTER III

45. The material in this section is drawn from passages on Jainism in several of the lectures that form the basis for other sections, particularly those on Hinduism and Buddhism.

46. Arthur Schopenhauer, "On the Sufferings of the World," *Studies in Pessimism: A Series of Essays,* trans. T. Bailey Saunders (London: Swan, Sonnenschein & Co., 1892). Bailey's somewhat fuller translation reads, "There are two things which make it impossible to believe that this world is the successful work of an all-wise, all-good, and, at the same time, all-powerful being; firstly, the misery which abounds in it everywhere; and secondly, the obvious imperfection of its highest product, man, who is a burlesque of what he should be. These things cannot be reconciled with any such belief. On the contrary, they are just the facts which support what I have been saying; they are our authority for viewing the world as the outcome of our own misdeeds, and therefore, as something that had better not have been."
47. The Gospel According to Saint Matthew, 6:28–29.
48. This section is drawn from a lecture delivered at Wainwright House on 21 November 1966 (L122) as the fourth part of a series entitled Symbolism and Mystical Experience. It has been released as "Hinduism," pt. 3 of *The Eastern Way,* vol. 3 of *The Joseph Campbell Audio Collection.*
49. This youth is almost certainly the young Jiddu Krishnamurti, whom Campbell had met originally on a transatlantic steamship in 1924. Campbell probably refrained from naming him out of respect for Krishnamurti's own reputation.
50. Lewis Mumford (1895–1990) was an architect, urban planner, and philosopher.
51. This section is drawn from a lecture delivered at Wainwright House on 28 November 1966 (L123) as the fifth and last part of a series entitled Symbolism and Mystical Experience. It has been released as "Buddhism," pt. 4 of *The Eastern Way,* vol. 3 of *The Joseph Campbell Audio Collection.* The section discussing the similarities between the story of the Buddha and that of Jesus was drawn from an answer that Campbell gave after a lecture on 23 January 1983 (L821).
52. T. S. Eliot, "Burnt Norton," *Four Quartets* (New York: Harcourt, Brace & Company, 1943), p. 15.
53. The Gospel According to Saint Thomas, Logion 113.
54. The Epistle of Paul the Apostle to the Philippians, 2:5–8.

55. Followers of this brand of Buddhism prefer to call it Theravāda Buddhism rather than Hinayāna ("small vessel"), which they consider derogatory.
56. The two snippets of verse, as much of the rest of the story of Hui-neng, are drawn from the Platform Sūtra of the Sixth Patriarch—the patriarch in question being Hui-neng himself.
57. This ceremony seems to have taken place during the International Congress for the History of Religions, which was held in Kyoto, Japan, in 1958.

ENVOY

58. Daisetz Teitaro Suzuki (1870–1966) was one of the most influential early proponents of Japanese Buddhism in the West. His books and lectures had a profound impact on Campbell. Among his many books was *An Introduction to Zen Buddhism,* with a foreword by C. G. Jung (New York: Philosophical Library, 1949).

A JOSEPH CAMPBELL BIBLIOGRAPHY

Following are the major books authored and edited by Joseph Campbell. Each entry gives bibliographic data concerning the first edition or, if applicable, the original date of publication along with the bibliographic data for the edition published by New World Library as part of the Collected Works of Joseph Campbell. For information concerning all other editions, please refer to the Complete Works of Joseph Campbell on the Joseph Campbell Foundation website (www.jcf.org).

Author

Where the Two Came to Their Father: A Navaho War Ceremonial Given by Jeff King. Bollingen Series I. With Maud Oakes and Jeff King. Richmond, VA: Old Dominion Foundation, 1943.

A Skeleton Key to Finnegans Wake: Unlocking James Joyce's Masterwork. With Henry Morton Robinson. 1944. Second edition, Novato, CA: New World Library, 2005.*

The Hero with a Thousand Faces. Bollingen Series xvii. 1949. Third edition, Novato, CA: New World Library, 2008.*

The Masks of God, 4 vols. New York: Viking Press, 1959–1968. Vol. 1, *Primitive Mythology,* 1959. Vol. 2, *Oriental Mythology,* 1962. Vol. 3, *Occidental Mythology,* 1964. Vol. 4, *Creative Mythology,* 1968.

The Flight of the Wild Gander: Explorations in the Mythological Dimension—Selected Essays 1944–1968. 1969. Third edition, Novato, CA: New World Library, 2002.*

Myths to Live By. 1972. Ebook edition, San Anselmo, CA: Joseph Campbell Foundation, 2011.

The Mythic Image. Bollingen Series c. Princeton, NJ: Princeton University Press, 1974.

The Inner Reaches of Outer Space: Metaphor as Myth and as Religion. 1986. Reprint, Novato, CA: New World Library, 2002.*

The Historical Atlas of World Mythology:

Vol. 1, *The Way of the Animal Powers.* New York: Alfred van der Marck Editions, 1983. Reprint in 2 pts. Part 1, *Mythologies of the Primitive Hunters and Gatherers.* New York: Alfred van der Marck Editions, 1988. Part 2, *Mythologies of the Great Hunt.* New York: Alfred van der Marck Editions, 1988.

Vol. 2, *The Way of the Seeded Earth,* 3 pts. Part 1, *The Sacrifice.* New York: Alfred van der Marck Editions, 1988. Part 2, *Mythologies of the Primitive Planters: The Northern Americas.* New York: Harper & Row Perennial Library, 1989. Part 3, *Mythologies of the Primitive Planters: The Middle and Southern Americas.* New York: Harper & Row Perennial Library, 1989.

The Power of Myth with Bill Moyers. With Bill Moyers. Edited by Betty Sue Flowers. New York: Doubleday, 1988.

Transformations of Myth Through Time. New York: Harper & Row, 1990.

The Hero's Journey: Joseph Campbell on His Life and Work. Edited by Phil Cousineau. 1990. Reprint, Novato, CA: New World Library, 2003.*

Reflections on the Art of Living: A Joseph Campbell Companion. Edited by Diane K. Osbon. New York: HarperCollins, 1991.

Mythic Worlds, Modern Words: On the Art of James Joyce. Edited by Edmund L. Epstein. 1993. Second edition, Novato, CA: New World Library, 2003.*

Baksheesh & Brahman: Asian Journals—India. Edited by Robin Larsen, Stephen Larsen, and Antony Van Couvering. 1995. Second edition, Novato, CA: New World Library, 2002.* [Reissued in paperback, together with *Sake & Satori,* in 2017; see *Asian Journals* entry below.]

The Mythic Dimension: Selected Essays 1959–1987. Edited by Antony Van Couvering. 1997. Second edition, Novato, CA: New World Library, 2007.*

Thou Art That. Edited by Eugene Kennedy. Novato, CA: New World Library, 2001.*

Sake & Satori: Asian Journals—Japan. Edited by David Kudler. Novato, CA: New World Library, 2002.* [Reissued in paperback, together with *Baksheesh & Brahman,* in 2017; see *Asian Journals* entry below.]

Myths of Light. Edited by David Kudler. Novato, CA: New World Library, 2003.*

Pathways to Bliss: Mythology and Personal Transformation. Ed. David Kudler. Novato, Calif.: New World Library, 2004.*

Mythic Imagination: Collected Short Fiction. Novato, CA: New World Library, 2012.*

Goddesses: Mysteries of the Feminine Divine. Edited by Safron Rossi. Novato, CA: New World Library, 2013.*

Romance of the Grail: The Magic and Mystery of Arthurian Myth. Edited by Evans Lansing Smith. Novato, CA: New World Library, 2015.*

Asian Journals: India and Japan. Combined paperback reissue of *Baksheesh & Brahman* and *Sake & Satori.* Book I: Baksheesh & Brahman—edited by Robin Larsen, Stephen Larsen, and Antony Van Couvering; book II: Sake & Satori—edited by David Kudler. Novato, CA: New World Library, 2017.*

The Ecstasy of Being: Mythology and Dance. Edited by Nancy Allison. Novato, CA: New World Library, 2017.*

* Published by New World Library as part of the Collected Works of Joseph Campbell.

Editor

Books edited and completed from the posthuma of Heinrich Zimmer:

Myths and Symbols in Indian Art and Civilization. Bollingen Series vi. New York: Pantheon, 1946.

The King and the Corpse. Bollingen Series xi. New York: Pantheon, 1948.

Philosophies of India. Bollingen Series xxvi. New York: Pantheon, 1951.

The Art of Indian Asia. Bollingen Series xxxix, 2 vols. New York: Pantheon, 1955.

Other books edited:

The Portable Arabian Nights. New York: Viking Press, 1951.

Papers from the Eranos Yearbooks. Bollingen Series xxx, 6 vols. Edited with R. F. C. Hull and Olga Froebe-Kapteyn. Translated by Ralph Manheim. Princeton: Princeton University Press, 1954–1969.

Myth, Dreams and Religion: Eleven Visions of Connection. New York: E. P. Dutton, 1970.

The Portable Jung. By C. G. Jung. Translated by R. F. C. Hull. New York: Viking Press, 1971.

My Life and Lives. By Rato Khyongla Nawang Losang. New York: E. P. Dutton, 1977.

INDEX

Page numbers of illustrations appear in italics.

A

B

C

D

E

J

K

L

M

S

Y

Z

ABOUT THE AUTHOR

JOSEPH CAMPBELL was an American author and teacher best known for his work in the field of comparative mythology. He was born in New York City in 1904, and from early childhood he became interested in mythology. He loved to read books about American Indian cultures, and frequently visited the American Museum of Natural History in New York, where he was fascinated by the museum's collection of totem poles. Campbell was educated at Columbia University, where he specialized in medieval literature, and, after earning a master's degree, continued his studies at universities in Paris and Munich. While abroad he was influenced by the art of Pablo Picasso and Henri Matisse, the novels of James Joyce and Thomas Mann, and the psychological studies of Sigmund Freud and Carl Jung. These encounters led to Campbell's theory that all myths and epics are linked in the human psyche, and that they are cultural manifestations of the universal need to explain social, cosmological, and spiritual realities.

After a period in California, where he encountered John Steinbeck and the biologist Ed Ricketts, he taught at the Canterbury School, and then, in 1934, joined the literature department at Sarah Lawrence College, a post he retained for many years. During the 1940s and '50s, he helped Swami

Nikhilananda to translate the *Upanishads* and *The Gospel of Sri Ramakrishna.* He also edited works by the German scholar Heinrich Zimmer on Indian art, myths, and philosophy. In 1944, with Henry Morton Robinson, Campbell published *A Skeleton Key to Finnegans Wake.* His first original work, *The Hero with a Thousand Faces,* came out in 1949 and was immediately well received; in time, it became acclaimed as a classic. In this study of the "myth of the hero," Campbell asserted that there is a single pattern of heroic journey and that all cultures share this essential pattern in their various heroic myths. In his book he also outlined the basic conditions, stages, and results of the archetypal hero's journey.

Joseph Campbell died in 1987. In 1988, a series of television interviews with Bill Moyers, *The Power of Myth,* introduced Campbell's views to millions of people.

ABOUT THE JOSEPH CAMPBELL FOUNDATION

THE JOSEPH CAMPBELL FOUNDATION (JCF) is a nonprofit corporation that continues the work of Joseph Campbell, exploring the fields of mythology and comparative religion. The Foundation is guided by three principal goals:

First, the Foundation preserves, protects, and perpetuates Campbell's pioneering work. This includes cataloging and archiving his works, developing new publications based on his works, directing the sale and distribution of his published works, protecting copyrights to his works, and increasing awareness of his works by making them available in digital formats on JCF's Web site.

Second, the Foundation promotes the study of mythology and comparative religion. This involves implementing and/or supporting diverse mythological education programs, supporting and/or sponsoring events designed to increase public awareness, donating Campbell's archived works (principally to the Joseph Campbell and Marija Gimbutas Archive and Library), and utilizing JCF's Web site as a forum for relevant cross-cultural dialogue.

Third, the Foundation helps individuals enrich their lives by participating in a series of programs, including our global, Internet-based Associates program, our local international network of Mythological Roundtables, and our periodic Joseph Campbell related events and activities.

www.jcf.org

NEW WORLD LIBRARY is dedicated to publishing books and other media that inspire and challenge us to improve the quality of our lives and the world.

We are a socially and environmentally aware company, and we strive to embody the ideals presented in our publications. We recognize that we have an ethical responsibility to our customers, our staff members, and our planet.

We serve our customers by creating the finest publications possible on personal growth, creativity, spirituality, wellness, and other areas of emerging importance. We serve New World Library employees with generous benefits, significant profit sharing, and constant encouragement to pursue their most expansive dreams.

As a member of the Green Press Initiative, we print an increasing number of books with soy-based ink on 100 percent postconsumer-waste recycled paper. Also, we power our offices with solar energy and contribute to nonprofit organizations working to make the world a better place for us all.

Our products are available in bookstores everywhere.
For our catalog, please contact:

New World Library
14 Pamaron Way, Novato, California 94949

Phone: 415-884-2100 or 800-972-6657
Catalog requests: Ext. 50
Orders: Ext. 52
Fax: 415-884-2199
Email: escort@newworldlibrary.com

To subscribe to our electronic newsletter, visit
www.newworldlibrary.com

3,183
trees were saved

HELPING TO PRESERVE OUR ENVIRONMENT

New World Library uses 100% postconsumer-waste recycled paper for our books whenever possible, even if it costs more. During 2010 this choice saved the following precious resources:

ENERGY	WASTEWATER	GREENHOUSE GASES	SOLID WASTE
22 MILLION BTU	600,000 GAL.	750,000 LB.	200,000 LB.

www.newworldlibrary.com

Environmental impact estimates were made using the Environmental Defense Fund Paper Calculator @ www.papercalculator.org.